OH DAD, POOR DAD,
MAMMA'S HUNG YOU IN THE CLOSET
AND I'M FEELIN' SO SAD

ALSO BY ARTHUR KOPIT

The Day the Whores Came Out to Play Tennis
and Other Plays

Indians

OH DAD, POOR DAD, MAMMA'S HUNG YOU IN THE CLOSET AND I'M FEELIN' SO SAD

A Pseudoclassical Tragifarce in a Bastard French Tradition

By ARTHUR L. KOPIT

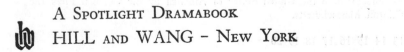

A SPOTLIGHT DRAMABOOK

HILL AND WANG – NEW YORK

Standard Book Number (clothbound edition): 8090-7420-6
Standard Book Number (paperback edition): 8090-1202-2

Library of Congress Catalog Card Number: 60-13996

FIRST DRAMABOOK PRINTING AUGUST 1960

Manufactured in the United States of America by the Colonial Press Inc.,
Clinton, Massachusetts.

13 14 15 16 17 18 19 20

To Maraki:
   For the abandon of her excitement
   in telling a simple story.

INTRODUCTION

WHEN *Oh Dad, Poor Dad* opened at Agassiz Theatre in Cambridge on January 7 of this year, it was accorded a stunning reception both by audiences and by the Boston press. A complex play, at once moving and hilarious, it called forth both vast enthusiasm and a great variety of interpretation. Most reactions agreed that Madame Rosepettle's view of life was grotesque, for example, but the *Christian Science Monitor* had "a curious sense that" Kopit "is half-convinced she is right." The excitement the play aroused was not unexpected. By the time of his graduation in 1959, Arthur Kopit had established himself as Harvard's most successful undergraduate playwright. During his last three years in college seven of his plays were performed in Cambridge, four in major undergraduate productions, three in private productions in Dunster House. *Oh Dad,* the culmination of his swift development, was written while he was on a Shaw Travelling Fellowship, a special postgraduate course of study, which was awarded him by the University. That he had taken courses in Engineering Sciences and, in the formal language of the award, was to study "Engineering and Applied Physics" abroad is a commentary on the diversity of his interests.

A disciplined fluency was apparent in his first play, *The Questioning of Nick*, written for the Dunster House Drama Workshop in the spring of 1957. Kopit often does his best work when a play, which has been thought out in advance, is written quickly. *Nick,* finished in three or four days, emerged a finely fashioned, realistic study of a high school athlete's interrogation in police headquarters. The boy's breakdown was foreshadowed in his flashes of humorous bravado, and the play's structure and language were

9

shaped by the presentation of Nick and the exploration of his personality. His last speech wound up simultaneously the closely connected strands of character, action, and language. The following fall *Nick* was awarded first prize in a playwriting contest and produced at Leverett House. It was performed again in 1959 on television by the Harvard Dramatic Club.

Although Kopit's plays are carefully planned, they do not originate with a preconceived idea of a kind of play he would like to write. They take their departure from an experience, or an observed character, or potentially dramatic situation, and as a result they express his special way of seeing and have their special tone of voice. The background of *Nick*, for example, was drawn from his experience playing basketball in high school. But his particular ability to transform a fragment of experience into something vividly different was revealed in *On the Runway of Life You Never Know What's Coming Off Next*. This play, produced in 1958 by the Harvard Dramatic Club, was about a precocious fifteen-year-old boy who contrived to get himself adopted as an orphan by two good-hearted carnival strippers. One of the women, Nefertiti, whom the boy annoys with a peashooter during her act, actually owed her particular inflections of voice to Kopit's friend Sallie Bingham, whose Southern accent he had admired and reproduced. When she appeared in the production, she appropriately brought to life the hilarious and outrageous metaphor herself.

It was in two plays written for performance during the annual Dunster Christmas weekend, however, that he experimented further in developing the humor of *On the Runway* into something even more wildly imaginative. For a take-off on Westerns, *Don Juan in Texas* (written with Wally Lawrence), Kopit contributed to the cast of characters "Two hundred dancing geisha girls," "Two cows, one bull, preferably brown," and "Two cactus plants" that "do not speak." He was also responsible for working into the farcical framework a comic resurrection scene and the strikingly pathetic farewell of the incompetent hero, an itinerant soap salesman mistaken for Billy the Kid. Elements of parody, frequent in *Oh Dad*, began to appear in Kopit's second Christmas play, *Across the River and into the Jungle*. There polka-dot natives, their pots hastening to a boil, joined their hapless victims in the chorus of Noel Coward's "I'll See You Again," and one of the characters finally completed a single sentence—which had been years in the writing and was to "be published in *Esquire* as a 'work in progress' "—satirizing Hemingway and the opening of *A Farewell to Arms*: "In the late summer of that year we lived in a hut in a tree on a mountain that looked across the river and the plain and the valley to another mountain with a hut in a tree."

The serious side of Kopit's writing reappeared, darker and intensified, in three plays either written or begun in the summer before his senior year. *Aubade*, an hour-long monologue for an actress-dancer, explored the nature of love and anticipated the monologue in the third scene of *Oh Dad*. *Sing to Me Through Open Windows* was a strange and delicate mood play about a boy, a retired magician, and a clown. Both plays, with original musical scores by two undergraduate friends of Kopit, Victor Ziskin and Thomas Beveridge, were performed last year in Dunster House under the title *Duet*. The third, *To Dwell in a Palace of Strangers*, was a full-length play about a mysterious intruder from the past who returns to disrupt the life of a former friend.

But particularly interesting was the fact that many of the carnival references of *On the Runway* were recapitulated within the melancholy world of *Sing to Me* with their distortions now appearing grotesque rather than comic. The mock circus barker scene was a bitter reversal of a similar passage in the earlier play. The juxtaposition of the two plays really suggests the method of *Oh Dad*. In a sense, the form of *Oh Dad* is the logical fusion of the comic and the serious facets of Kopit's imagination. By taking the techniques he experimented with earlier and developing them simultaneously, it plays the two related attitudes in counterpoint.

The form of *Oh Dad*, inherent in the nature of Kopit's writing, is also, and properly, in a style that is immediately contemporary. The broadly comic treatment of serious, almost terrifying subject matter Shaw had exaggerated out of Chekhov in *Heartbreak House*; Giraudoux, Beckett, Anouilh, Ionesco, and Duerrenmatt have developed this dramatic method with great virtuosity in their own ways. Although *Oh Dad* is a response to their plays, it and all of these plays are a response to a particular time and to the common problems of the theatre.

The modern world has seen too much pain to view pain with the detachment that tragedy, if it were otherwise possible, would require, and actual disaster has been too familiar for the suspension of disbelief that its representation in art must assume. The modern tragicomic play has become the contemporary dramatist's finest solution, with the comic framework providing the necessary perspective for the darker insights and asserting with special force a sense of distance and the reminder that art is not intended to be literally true. What Kopit calls "the bastard French tradition," in which *Oh Dad* takes its highly individual place, is also exciting, because it represents a new assault upon the theatre as a laboratory for case histories or as a loudspeaker for transient propaganda. In an effort to attain scope for language and suggestions of the tragic, the new tradition is making another of those periodic attempts to blast apart the stubborn structure of prose realism and claim the theatre once again as the domain of "imaginary forces," the kingdom of the extraordinary it has always been in its times of ascendance.

The journey of former Harvard students from the Square to Broadway is by now a familiar one to the American theatre, for Edward Sheldon, Philip Barry, Eugene O'Neill, Robert E. Sherwood, and Robert Anderson have traveled it before. Arthur Kopit follows them now, his luggage crammed with the stuff of his personal imagination: his wit, the sureness of his verbal gift, his instinctive theatricality, and those darting plunges into the abyss of the heart that is always receding beneath the wild and brilliant surface of *Oh Dad*.

GAYNOR F. BRADISH

Harvard University
April 30, 1960

OH DAD, POOR DAD,
MAMMA'S HUNG YOU IN THE CLOSET
AND I'M FEELIN' SO SAD

Characters

MADAME ROSEPETTLE
JONATHAN ROSEPETTLE
ROSALIE
COMMODORE ROSEABOVE
ROSALINDA THE FISH
TWO VENUS'-FLYTRAPS
A CUCKOO CLOCK
VARIOUS BELLBOYS

The play is in three scenes, without intermission.
The setting is a hotel in HAVANA, CUBA.

SCENE 1

A *lavish hotel room in Havana, Cuba. Downstage center French windows open onto a large balcony that juts out over the audience. Upstage center are the doors to the master bedroom. At stage left is the door to another bedroom, while at stage right is the door to the suite itself. On one of the walls is hung a glass case with a red fire axe inside it and a sign over it that reads, "In Case of Emergency, Break."*

The door to the suite opens and BELLBOYS NUMBER ONE *and* Two *enter carrying a coffin.*

WOMAN'S VOICE [*From off stage*]. Put it in the bedroom!

BELLBOYS NUMBER ONE AND TWO [*Together*]. The bedroom. [BELLBOY NUMBER ONE *starts toward the bedroom at stage left.* BELLBOY NUMBER TWO *starts toward the bedroom at upstage center. The handles come off the coffin. It falls to the floor. The* BELLBOYS *freeze with horror.*]

WOMAN'S VOICE [*Still off stage*]. Fools!

Enter MADAME ROSEPETTLE, *dressed in black, a veil hiding her face.* JONATHAN, *a boy seventeen years old but dressed like a child of ten, enters directly behind her. He follows her about the room like a small helpless puppy trailing his master.*

MADAME ROSEPETTLE. Morons! Imbeciles!

15

BELLBOY NUMBER ONE. Uh . . . *which* bedroom, madame?

BELLBOY NUMBER TWO. Yes. *Which* bedroom?

MADAME ROSEPETTLE. *Which bedroom!?* They have the nerve to ask, which bedroom? The *master* bedroom, of course. Which bedroom did you think? [*The* BELLBOYS *smile ashamedly, bow, pick up the coffin and carry it toward the master bedroom.*] Gently! [*They open the bedroom doors.* MADAME ROSEPETTLE *lowers her face as blindingly bright sunlight pours out from the room.*] People have no respect for coffins nowadays. They think nothing of the dead. [*Short pause.*] I wonder what the dead think of them? Agh! The world is growing dismal.

The BELLBOYS *reappear in the doorway, the coffin in their hands.*

BELLBOY NUMBER ONE. Uh . . . begging your pardon, ma-dame, but . . . but . . .

MADAME ROSEPETTLE. Speak up! Speak up!

BELLBOY NUMBER ONE. Well, you see . . .

BELLBOY NUMBER TWO. You see . . . we were curious.

BELLBOY NUMBER ONE. Yes. Curious. That is . . .

BELLBOY NUMBER TWO. What we mean to say is . . .

BELLBOY NUMBER ONE. Just *where* in your bedroom would you like us to put it?

MADAME ROSEPETTLE. Next to the *bed,* of course!

BELLBOYS NUMBER ONE AND TWO. *Of course.*
                    [*Exit,* BELLBOYS NUMBER ONE *and* TWO.

MADAME ROSEPETTLE. *Fools.*

There is a rap on the door to the suite.

BELLBOY NUMBER THREE [*Off stage*]. The dictaphone, madame.

MADAME ROSEPETTLE. Ah, splendid.

BELLBOY NUMBER THREE *enters carrying a dictaphone on a silver tray and black drapes under his arm.* BELLBOYS NUMBER ONE *and* TWO *leave the bedroom and exit from the suite, bowing fearfully to Madame Rosepettle as they leave.*

BELLBOY NUMBER THREE. Where would you like it placed?

MADAME ROSEPETTLE. Great gods! Are you all the same? The center table, naturally! One never dictates one's memoirs from *anywhere* but the middle of a room. Any nincompoop knows that.

BELLBOY NUMBER THREE. It must have slipped my mind.

MADAME ROSEPETTLE. You flatter yourself. [*He puts the dictaphone and drapes down on the table.*]

BELLBOY NUMBER THREE. Will there be anything else?

MADAME ROSEPETTLE. *Will there be anything else*, he asks!? Will there be anything else? Of course there'll be something else. There's *always* something else. That's one of the troubles with Life.

BELLBOY NUMBER THREE. Sorry, madame.

MADAME ROSEPETTLE. So am I. [*Pause.*] Oh, this talk is getting us nowhere. Words are precious. On bellboys they're a waste. And so far you have thoroughly wasted my time.

BELLBOY NUMBER THREE. Madame, this must end. I can take no more. I will have you know I am not a *common* bellboy. I am a lieutenant. Notice, if you will, the finely embroidered stripes on my hand-tailored sleeve. I am a lieutenant, madame, and being a lieutenant am in charge of other bellboys and thereby entitled to a little more respect from you.

MADAME ROSEPETTLE. Well, *you* may consider yourself a lieutenant, lieutenant, but *I* consider you a *bore!* If you're going to insist upon pulling rank, however, I'll have you know that I am a tourist. Notice, if you will, the money. And being a tourist I am in charge of you. Remember that and I'll mail you another stripe when I leave. As for "respect," we'll have none of that around here. We've got too many important things to do. Right, Albert? [*Jonathan tries to speak but cannot.*] Rrrright, Albert?

JONATHAN. Ra . . . ra . . . ra . . . ra-right.

MADAME ROSEPETTLE. You may begin by picking up the drapes you so ingeniously dropped in a lump on my table, carrying them to the master bedroom and tacking them over the windowpanes. I don't wear black in the tropics for my health, my boy. I'm in mourning. And since the problems confronting civilization are ultimately moral ones, while I'm here in Havana no single speck of sunlight shall enter and brighten the mournful gloom of my heart. [*Short pause.*] At least, not while I'm in my bedroom. Well, go on, lieutenant, go on. Forward to the field of battle, head high. Tack the drapes across my windows, and when my room is black, call me in.

BELLBOY NUMBER THREE. Yes, madame.
[*He picks up the drapes and walks into the master bedroom.*

MADAME ROSEPETTLE. In Buenos Aires the lieutenant clicked his heels when leaving. That's the trouble with these revolutionaries. No regard for the duties of rank. Remind me, Edward, to decrease my usual tip. [JONATHAN *takes a pad of paper out of his pocket and writes with a pencil he has tied on a cord about his neck. To the hallway.*] Well, come in, come in. Don't just stand there with your mouths hanging open.

Bellboys Number One *and* Two *and* Four *enter pushing heavy trunks before them.*

Bellboy Number One. Where would you like the stamp collection, madame?

Madame Rosepettle. Ah, your fantastic stamp collection, Robinson. Where should it be put?

Jonathan. Uh . . . uh . . . uh . . .

Madame Rosepettle. Oh, stop stammering and speak up! They're only bellboys.

Jonathan. Uh . . . um . . . um . . . ma . . . ma . . . ma-ma-ma-ma-ma . . . ma—maybe . . . in . . . in . . . in . . .

Madame Rosepettle. Will you stop this infernal stammering? You know what I think about it! I said, where would you like your fantastic stamp collection put? God knows it's a simple enough question. If you can't muster the nerve to answer, at least point. [*He points to a bureau in the room.*] The bottom drawer of the bureau. And be careful not to get your fingers on them. They stick. [*The* Bellboys *go to the bureau, open the drawer, and dump hundreds of loose stamps that had been in the trunk into the drawer.* Madame Rosepettle *dips her hand into the drawer and plucks out three stamps. She offers one to each of the* Bellboys.] Here, for your trouble: 1903 Borneo, limited edition. Very rare. Almost priceless.

The Bellboys *look disappointedly at their tips.* Bellboy Number Three *returns from the master bedroom.*

Bellboy Number Three. I'm terribly sorry, madame, but I find that—

MADAME ROSEPETTLE. I wondered when you'd ask. [*She takes a huge hammer from her purse and hands it to him.*]

BELLBOY NUMBER THREE. Thank you, madame. Thank you. [*He turns nervously and starts to leave.*]

MADAME ROSEPETTLE. Bellboy? [*He stops.*] The nails.

BELLBOY NUMBER THREE [*Flustered by his forgetfulness*]. Yes, of course. How foolish of me. [*She reaches into her purse again and takes out a fistful of nails which she promptly dumps into his hands.*]

MADAME ROSEPETTLE. Keep the extras.

[*He exits into the master bedroom.* [*To Jonathan.*] In Buenos Aires the lieutenant came equipped with a pneumatic drill. Remind me, Albert dearest, to cut this man's tip entirely. [JONATHAN *scribbles on his pad. To the other* BELLBOYS.] Well?

BELLBOY NUMBER TWO. The . . . uh . . . coin collection, madame. Where would you like it put?

MADAME ROSEPETTLE. Your fabulous coin collection, Edward. Where should they put it?

JONATHAN. Uh . . . uh . . . I . . . I . . . I tha . . . tha . . . tha-think—

MADAME ROSEPETTLE. What is wrong with your tongue? Can't you talk like a normal human being without showering this room with your inarticulate spit!?

JONATHAN [*Completely flustered*]. I-I-I-I-I . . . I . . . da . . . da . . . don't . . .

MADAME ROSEPETTLE. Oh, all right, stick out your paw and point. [*He thrusts out his trembling hand and points again to the bureau.*]

JONATHAN. If . . . if . . . if . . . if they . . . if they would . . . be so . . . kind.

MADAME ROSEPETTLE. Of course they would! They're bellboys. Remember that. It's your first lesson in Life for the day. [*To the* BELLBOYS.] Next to the bottom drawer, bellboys. And make sure none of them gets in with his fantastic collection of stamps. [*From the master bedroom can be heard the sound of* BELLBOY NUMBER THREE *smashing nails into the wall. While the other* BELLBOYS *are busy dumping hundreds of loose coins into the bureau,* MADAME ROSEPETTLE *walks to the bedroom door and opens it, shielding her eyes from the blinding light.*] Don't bang, my boy. Don't bang. That's not the way. Just tap. It takes longer, I will admit, but the effect is far more satisfactory on one's auditory nerves—and my ears, you see, are extremely sensitive. [*To Jonathan.*] The lieutenant in Buenos Aires had a muffler on his drill. Remind me, Robinson darling, to have this man fired first thing in the morning. He'll never do. [JONATHAN *scratches a large "X" on his pad. The* BELLBOYS, *having finished dumping the coins, stand awaiting a tip.* MADAME ROSEPETTLE *goes to the drawer and takes out three coins. To* BELLBOY NUMBER ONE.] Here, for your trouble: a little something. It's a Turkish piaster . . . 1876. Good year for piasters. [*To* BELLBOY NUMBER TWO.] And for you an . . . an 1889 Danzig gulden. Worth a fortune, my boy. A *small* fortune, I will admit, but nevertheless, a fortune. [*To* BELLBOY NUMBER FOUR.] And for you we have a . . . a . . . a 1959 DIME!! *Edward* . . . what is a dime doing in here? Fegh! [*She flings the dime to the ground as if it had been handled by lepers. The* BELLBOYS *leap to get it.*]

JONATHAN [*Sadly*]. Some . . . some . . . someday it will be . . . as rare as the others.

MADAME ROSEPETTLE. Someday! *Someday!* That's the trouble with you, Edward. Always an optimist. I trust you have no more such currency contaminating your fabulous collection. H'm, Albert? Do I assume correctly? H'm? Do I? H'm? Do I? H'm? Do I?

JONATHAN. Ya . . . yes.

MADAME ROSEPETTLE. Splendid. Then I'll give you your surprise for the day.

JONATHAN. Na . . . now?

MADAME ROSEPETTLE. Yes, now.

JONATHAN. In . . . in . . . front of . . . *them?*

MADAME ROSEPETTLE. Turn your backs, bellboys. [*She digs into her handbag and picks out a coin in a velvet box.*] Here, Edward, my sweet. The rarest of all coins for your rarest of all collections. A 1372 Javanese Yen-Sen.

JONATHAN [*Excitedly*]. How . . . how . . . how ma-many were . . . ma-minted?

MADAME ROSEPETTLE. None.

JONATHAN. Na-none?

MADAME ROSEPETTLE. I made it myself. [*She squeezes his hand.*] So glad you like it. [*She turns to the* BELLBOYS.] You may turn around now. [*They turn around as a unit.*] Well, who has the—? [*She stares in horror at the door to the master bedroom. The tapping can clearly be heard. She goes to the door, shielding her eyes from the now less powerful glare.*] You are tapping and not banging, which is good, but when you tap please tap with some sort of rhythm, which is, you see, much better. [*She smiles acidly and closes the door.*] The lieutenant in Buenos Aires, Robinson. The lieutenant in Buenos Aires. Do you remember him? Do you remember the rhythm he had? Oh, the way he shook when he drilled. I fairly danced that day. [*Reminiscent pause.*] Make note, Robinson. This man must be barred from all hotels, everywhere. *Everywhere!* [JONATHAN *retraces his "X" with a hard, firm stroke as if he were carving a figure on stone.*] Now where was I? Oh, yes. Forgive me, but my mind, of late, has been wandering. The books, bellboys. The books! [*The* BELLBOYS *push a large trunk forward.*]

JONATHAN. Ca . . . ca . . . could they . . . open it . . . I . . . I-I wonder?

MADAME ROSEPETTLE. You want to see them, eh Albert? You really want to see them again? That badly? You really want to see them again, that badly?

JONATHAN [*Trying very hard not to stutter*]. Yyyyesssssss.

MADAME ROSEPETTLE [*Very dramatically*]. Then let the trunk be opened! [*They open the trunk. Hundreds of books fall onto the floor in a cloud of dust.* JONATHAN *falls on top of them like a starved man upon food.*]

JONATHAN [*Emotionally*]. Tra-Tra . . . Trollope . . . Ha-Haggard . . . Dau-Dau-Daudet . . . Gautier . . . Tur-Tur-Tur-genev . . . ma-ma-my old fra-fra . . . friends. [*He collapses over them like a lover over his loved one.*]

MADAME ROSEPETTLE. Enough, Albert. Come. Off your knees. Rise from your books and sing of love.

JONATHAN. But I . . . I ca-can't . . . sing.

MADAME ROSEPETTLE. Well, stand up anyway. [*He rises sadly.*] Now, where are my plants?

BELLBOY NUMBER TWO. Plants?

MADAME ROSEPETTLE. Yes. My plants. Where are they? [BELL-BOY NUMBER FOUR *whispers something in* BELLBOY NUMBER TWO's *ear.*]

BELLBOY NUMBER TWO [*Laughing nervously*]. Oh. I . . . I . . . [*He laughs again, more nervously.*] I didn't realize . . . they were . . . plants.

MADAME ROSEPETTLE. What did you *think* they were?

BELLBOY NUMBER FOUR. We have them, madame. Outside.

BELLBOY NUMBER TWO. Yes. Outside.

BELLBOY NUMBER FOUR. Should we . . . bring them in?

MADAME ROSEPETTLE. Of course you should bring them in! Do you think they *enjoy* waiting out there in the hall? *Fools.*

BELLBOYS NUMBER TWO AND FOUR [*Together, weakly*]. Yes . . . madame.

They exit and return immediately carrying two large black-draped "things" before them at arm's length.

MADAME ROSEPETTLE. Ah, splendid. Splendid. Set them on the porch, if you will. [*They go out to the porch and set them down.*] Uh . . . not so close together. They fight. [*The* BELLBOYS *move the* PLANTS *apart.*]

BELLBOY NUMBER FOUR [*Weakly*]. Should we . . . uncover them?

MADAME ROSEPETTLE. No. That will be fine. Let the poor things rest awhile.

BELLBOYS NUMBER TWO AND FOUR [*Together, weakly*]. Yes . . . madame.

MADAME ROSEPETTLE. Now . . . who has my fish? [*All* BELL-BOYS *look toward the door.*]

A VOICE [*From outside the door*]. I have it, madame.

Enter BELLBOY NUMBER FIVE *carrying, at arm's length, an object covered by a black cloth. He wears large, thick, well-padded gloves—the sort a snake trainer might wear when handling a newly caught cobra.*

MADAME ROSEPETTLE [*With love in her voice*]. Ah, bring it here. Put it here, by the dictaphone. Near my memoirs. Bring it here, bellboy. Set it gently, then lift the shawl.

JONATHAN [*Staring sadly at his books*]. Sho-Sho-Sholo-Sholokhov . . . Alain-Fournier . . . Alighieri . . . ma-my ffffriends. [*The* BELLBOY *sets the object down.*]

MADAME ROSEPETTLE. The black shawl of mourning, bellboy. Remove it, if you will. Lift it off and drape it near its side. But gently. Gently. Gently as she goes. [*The* BELLBOY *lifts off the shawl. Revealed is a fish bowl with a* FISH *and a cat's skeleton inside.*] Ah, I see you fed it today. [*She reaches into her handbag and extracts a pair of long tongs. She plucks the skeleton from the fish bowl.*] Siamese, I presume.

BELLBOY NUMBER FOUR. No, madame. Alley.

MADAME ROSEPETTLE. WHAT!? A *common alley cat?* Just who do you think I am? What kind of fish do you think I have? *Alley cat! Alley cat!* The idea! In Buenos Aires, I'll have you know, Rosalinda was fed nothing but Siamese *kittens*, which are even more tender than Siamese cats. *That's* what I call consideration! Edward, make note: we will dismiss this creature from the bellboy squad *first thing in the morning!* [JONATHAN *scribbles on his pad.*]

BELLBOY NUMBER FOUR. Madame, please, there were no Siamese cats.

MADAME ROSEPETTLE. There are *always* Siamese cats!

BELLBOY NUMBER FOUR. Not in Havana.

MADAME ROSEPETTLE. Then you should have flown to Buenos Aires. I would have paid the way. Give me back your 1903 Borneo, limited. (I'll bet you've made it sticky.) [*He hands back the stamp.*] You can keep your Danzig gulden. It's not worth a thing except in Danzig, and hardly a soul uses anything but traveler's checks there anyhow! Shows you should never trust me.

BELLBOY NUMBER FOUR. Madame, *please.* I have a wife.

MADAME ROSEPETTLE. And *I* have a fish. I dare say there are half a million men in Cuba with wives. But show me another woman in Cuba with a silver piranha fish and then you'll be showing me something. Your marital status does not impress me, sir. You are common, do you hear? Common! While my piranha fish is *rare.* Now green piranhas can eat alley cats if they like; and red piranhas, I've been told, will often eat alley cats, tomcats, and even dogs; but my silver piranha has been weaned on Siamese, and Siamese it will be, sir. Siamese it will be. Now get out. All of you. There is much to do. Right, Albert?

JONATHAN. Ra . . . ra . . . ra . . . ra . . .

MADAME ROSEPETTLE. *Right,* Albert!?

JONATHAN. Ra-right.

ROSALINDA THE FISH [*Sadly*]. Glump.

MADAME ROSEPETTLE. Oh, dear thing. You can just tell she's
not feeling up to snuff. *Someone will pay for this!*
　Enter LIEUTENANT *of the bellboys from the bedroom.*

BELLBOY NUMBER THREE. Well, I'm finished.

MADAME ROSEPETTLE. You certainly are, *monsieur lieutenant.*
You certainly are.

BELLBOY NUMBER THREE. I beg your pardon?

MADAME ROSEPETTLE. Make note, Edward. First thing in the
morning we speak to the chef. Subject: Siamese cats—kittens if
possible, though I seriously doubt it here. And make a further
note, Albert, my darling. Let's see if we can't get our cats on the
American Plan, while we're at it. [JONATHAN *scribbles on his pad
of paper.*]

BELLBOY NUMBER THREE. Madame, is there something I can—?

MADAME ROSEPETTLE. QUIET! And put that hammer down.
[*He puts it down. She puts it back in her purse.*] You have all
behaved rudely. If the sunset over Guanabacoa Bay were not so
full of magenta and wisteria blue I'd leave this place tonight.
But the sunset *is* full of magneta and wisteria blue, to say nothing
of cadmium orange and cerise, and so I think I'll stay. Therefore
beware, bellboys. Madame Rosepettle will have much to do.
Right, Robinson? [JONATHAN *opens his mouth to speak but no
words come out.*] I said, *right Robinson?* [*Again he tries to speak,
and again no words come out.*] RIGHT, ROBINSON!? [*He
nods.*] There's your answer. Now get out and leave us alone.
[*They start to exit.*] No. Wait. [*They stop.*] A question before you
go. The yacht in the harbor. The pink one with the lilacs draped
about the railing. One hundred and eighty-seven feet long, I'd
judge. Who owns it?

BELLBOY NUMBER ONE. Commodore Roseabove, madame. It's a pretty sloop.

MADAME ROSEPETTLE [*Distantly*]. Roseabove. I like that name.

BELLBOY NUMBER ONE. He's a strange man, madame. A man who knows no master but the sea.

MADAME ROSEPETTLE [*With a slight smile*]. Roseabove . . .

BELLBOY NUMBER ONE. A wealthy man but a gentleman, too. Why I've seen him with my own eyes toss *real silver dollars* to the native boats as he sailed into port. And when some poor diver came to the surface without a coin glimmering in his hand, Commodore Roseabove, without the slightest hesitation, dropped a dollar bill instead. Oh he's a well-loved man, madame. A true, true gentleman with a big, big heart. A man who knows no master but the sea. And even the sea, they say, is no match for the commodore and his yacht, which, as you know, is the largest yacht in Cuba.

MADAME ROSEPETTLE. And also the largest yacht in Haiti, Puerto Rico, Bermuda, the Dominican Republic, and West Palm Beach. I haven't checked the Virgin Islands yet. I thought I'd leave them till last. But I doubt if I'll find a larger one there. [*She laughs to herself.*] I take great pleasure, you see, in measuring yachts. My hobby, you might say.

BELLBOY NUMBER ONE. Your hubby, did you say?

MADAME ROSEPETTLE [*Viciously*]. Get out! Get out before I lose my temper! *Imbeciles!* FOOLS!
[*They exit, running.*
Edward, make note. First thing in the morning, we restaff this hotel. [JONATHAN *scribbles on his pad of paper.* MADAME ROSE-PETTLE *walks over to the French windows and stares wistfully out.*

There is a short silence before she speaks. Dreamily, with a slight smile.] Roseabove. I like that name.

ROSALINDA THE FISH [*Gleefully*]. Gleep.

MADAME ROSEPETTLE [*Fondly*]. Ah, listen. My lovely little fish. She, too, is feeling better already.

Curtain.

SCENE 2

The place is the same. The time, two weeks later. JONATHAN *is in the room with* ROSALIE, *a girl some two years older than he and dressed in sweet girlish pink.*

ROSALIE. But if you've been here two weeks, why haven't I seen you?

JONATHAN. I've . . . I've been in my room.

ROSALIE. All the time?

JONATHAN. Yes. . . . All the time.

ROSALIE. Well, you must get out sometimes. I mean, sometimes you simply must get out. You just couldn't stay inside all the time . . . could you?

JONATHAN. Yyyyyes.

ROSALIE. You never get out at all? I mean, never at all?

JONATHAN. Some-sometimes I do go out on the porch. M-Ma-Mother has some . . . Venus'-flytraps which she bra-brought back from the rain forests of Va-Va-Va-Venezuela. They're va-very rrrrrare and need a . . . a lot of sunshine. Well sir, she ka-keeps them on the porch and I . . . I feed them. Twice a day, too.

31

ROSALIE. Oh.

JONATHAN. Ma-Ma-Mother says everyone must have a vocation in life. [*With a slight nervous laugh.*] I ga-guess that's . . . my job.

ROSALIE. I don't think I've ever met anyone before who's fed . . . uh . . . Venus'-flytraps.

JONATHAN. Ma-Ma-Mother says I'm va-very good at it. That's what she . . . says. I'm va-very good at it. I . . . don't know . . . if . . . I am, but . . . that's . . . what she says so I . . . guess I am.

ROSALIE. Well, uh, what . . . what do you . . . feed them? You see, I've never met anyone before who's fed Venus'-flytraps so . . . that's why I don't know what . . . you're supposed to feed them.

JONATHAN [*Happy that she asked*]. Oh, I fa-feed them . . . l-l-lots of things. Ga-ga-green peas, chicken feathers, rubber bands. They're . . . not very fussy. They're . . . nice, that way. Ma-Ma-Mother says it it it ga-gives me a feeling of a-co-co-complishment. Iffffff you would . . . like to to see them I . . . could show them to you. It's . . . almost fa-feeding time. It is, and . . . and I could show them to you.

ROSALIE. No. That's all right. [JONATHAN *looks away, hurt.*] Well, how about later?

JONATHAN. Do-do-do you ra-really wwwwwant to see them?

ROSALIE. Yes. Yes I really think I would like to see them . . . later. If you'll show them to me then, I'd really like that. [JONATHAN *looks at her and smiles. There is an awkward silence while he stares at her thankfully.*] I still don't understand why you never go out. How can you just sit in——?

JONATHAN. Sometimes, when I'm on the porch . . . I do other things.

ROSALIE. *What?*

JONATHAN. Sa-sa-sometimes, when I'm . . . on the porch, you know, when I'm on the porch? Sssssssssome-times I . . . do *other things*, too.

ROSALIE. What sort of things? [JONATHAN *giggles.*] What sort of things do you do?

JONATHAN. Other things.

ROSALIE [*Coyly*]. What do you mean, "Other things"?

JONATHAN. Other things besides feeding my mother's plants. Other things besides that. That's what I mean. Other things besides that.

ROSALIE. What kind of things . . . *in particular?*

JONATHAN. Oh, watching.

ROSALIE. Watching?

JONATHAN. Yes. Like . . . watching.

ROSALIE. Watching what? [*He giggles.*] *Watching what!?*

JONATHAN. You. [*Short pause. She inches closer to him on the couch.*]

ROSALIE. What do you mean . . . watching me?

JONATHAN. I . . . watch you from the porch. That's what I mean. I watch you from the porch. I watch you a lot, too. Every day. It's . . . it's the truth. I . . . I swear it . . . is. I watch you ev-ry day. Do you believe me?

ROSALIE. Of course I believe you, Albert. Why—

JONATHAN. Jonathan!

ROSALIE. What?

JONATHAN. Jonathan. Ca-ca-call me Ja-Jonathan. That's my na-na-na——

ROSALIE. But your mother said your name was—

JONATHAN. Nooooo! Call . . . me Jonathan. Pa-pa-please?

ROSALIE. All right . . . Jonathan.

JONATHAN [*Excitedly*]. You *do* believe me! You rrrrreally do believe me. I-I-I can tell!

ROSALIE. Of course I believe you. Why shouldn't—?

JONATHAN. You want me to tell you how I watch you? You want me to tell you? I'll bet you'll na-never guess.

ROSALIE. How?

JONATHAN. *Guess.*

ROSALIE [*Ponders*]. Through a telescope?

JONATHAN. How did you guess?

Rosalie. I . . . I don't know. I was just joking. I didn't really think that was—

Jonathan. I'll bet everyone watches you through a telescope. I'll bet everyone you go out with watches you through a telescope. That's what I'll bet.

Rosalie. No. Not at all.

Jonathan. Well, that's how I watch you. Through a telescope.

Rosalie. I never would have guessed that—

Jonathan. I thought you were . . . ga-going to say I . . . I watch you with . . . with love in my eyes or some . . . thing like that. I didn't think you were going to guess that I . . . watch you through a telescope. I didn't think you were going to guess that I wa-watch you through a telescope on the fa-first guess, anyway. Not on the *first guess*.

Rosalie. Well, it was just a guess.

Jonathan [*Hopefully*]. Do you watch *me* through a telescope?

Rosalie. I never knew where your room was.

Jonathan. Now you know. Now will you watch me?

Rosalie. Well I . . . don't have a telescope.

Jonathan [*Getting more elated and excited*]. You can make one. That's how I got mine. I made it. Out of lenses and tubing. That's all you need. Lenses and tubing. Do you have any lenses?

Rosalie. No.

Jonathan. Do you have any tubing?

ROSALIE. No.

JONATHAN. Oh. [*Pause.*] Well, would you like me to tell you how I made mine in case you find some lenses and tubing? Would you like that?

ROSALIE [*Disinterestedly*]. Sure, Jonathan. I think that would be nice.

JONATHAN. Well, I made it out of lenses and tubing. The lenses I had because Ma-Ma-Mother gave me a set of lenses so I could see my stamps better. I have a fabulous collection of stamps, as well as a fantastic collection of coins and a simply unbelievable collection of books. Well sir, Ma-Ma-Mother gave me these lenses so I could see my stamps better. She suspected that some were fake so she gave me the lenses so I might be . . . able to see. You see? Well sir, I happen to have nearly a billion sta-stamps. So far I've looked closely at 1,352,769. I've discovered three actual fakes! Number 1,352,767 was a fake. Number 1,352,768 was a fake, and number 1,352,769 was a fake. They were stuck together. Ma-Mother made me feed them im-mediately to her flytraps. Well . . . [*He whispers.*] one day, when Mother wasn't looking . . . that is, when she was out, I heard an airplane flying. An airplane . . . somewhere . . . far away. It wasn't very loud, but still I heard it. An airplane. Flying . . . somewhere, far away. And I ran outside to the porch so that I might see what it looked like. The airplane. With hundreds of people inside it. Hundreds and hundreds and hundreds of people. And I thought to myself, if I could just see . . . if I could just see what they looked like, the people, sitting at their windows looking out . . . and flying. If I could see . . . *just* once . . . if I could see *just once* what they looked like . . . then I might . . . know what I . . . what I . . . [*Slight pause.*] So I . . . built a telescope in case the plane ever . . . came back again. The tubing came from an old blowgun [*He reaches behind the bureau and produces a huge blowgun, easily a foot larger than he.*] Mother brought back from her last hunting trip to Zanzibar. The lenses were the lenses she had given me for my stamps. So I built it. My telescope. A telescope so I might be able to see. And . . . [*He walks out to the porch.*] and . . . and I *could* see! I could! I COULD! I really could. For miles and miles I could see. For miles and miles and *miles!* [*He begins to lift it up to look through but stops, for some reason, before he's brought it up to his eye.*] Only . . . [*He hands it to* ROSALIE. *She takes it eagerly and scans the horizon and the sky. She hands it back to him.*]

ROSALIE [*With annoyance*]. There's nothing out there to see.

JONATHAN [*Sadly.*] I know. That's the trouble. You take the time to build a telescope that can sa-see for miles, then there's nothing out there to see. Ma-Mother says it's a lesson in Life. [*Pause.*] But I'm not sorry I built my telescope. And you know why? Because I saw you. Even if I didn't see anything else, I did see you. And . . . and I'm . . . very glad. [ROSALIE *moves slightly closer to him on the couch. She moistens her lips.*] I . . . I remember, you were standing across the way in your penthouse garden playing blind man's buff with ten little children. [*After a short pause, fearfully.*] Are . . . are they by any chance . . . *yours?*

ROSALIE [*Sweetly*]. Oh, I'm not married.

JONATHAN. Oh!

ROSALIE. I'm a baby sitter.

JONATHAN [*With obvious relief*]. Oh.

ROSALIE. I work for the people who own the penthouse.

JONATHAN. I've never seen them around.

ROSALIE. I've never seen them either. They're never home. They just mail me a check every week and tell me to make sure I keep the children's names straight.

JONATHAN. If you could tell me which way they went I could find them with my telescope. It can see for miles.

ROSALIE. They must love children very much. I'll bet she's a marvelous woman. [*Pause.*] There's going to be another one, too! Another child is coming! I got a night letter last night.

JONATHAN. By airplane?

ROSALIE. I don't know.

JONATHAN. I bet it was. I can't see at night. Ma-Mother can but I can't. I'll bet that's when the planes fly.

ROSALIE [*Coyly*]. If you like, I'll read you the letter. I have it with me. [*She unbuttons the top of her blouse and turns around in a coquettish manner to take the letter from her brassiere. Reading.*] "Have had another child. Sent it yesterday. Will arrive tomorrow. Call it Cynthia."

JONATHAN. That will make eleven. That's an awful lot of children to take care of. I'll bet it must be wonderful.

ROSALIE. They do pay very well.

JONATHAN. They pay you?

ROSALIE. Of course . . . What did you think? [*Pause. Softly, seductively.*] Jonathan? [*He does not answer but seems lost in thought. With a feline purr.*] Jonathan?

JONATHAN. Yyyyyes?

ROSALIE. It gets very lonesome over there. The children go to sleep early and the parents are never home so I'm always alone. Perhaps . . . well Jonathan, I thought that perhaps you might . . . visit me.

JONATHAN. Well . . . well . . . well, you . . . you see . . . I . . . I . . .

ROSALIE. We could spend the evenings together . . . at my place. It gets so lonesome there, you know what I mean? I mean, I don't know what to do. I get so lonesome there.

JONATHAN. Ma-ma-ma-maybe you . . . you can . . . come over . . . here? Maybe you you can do . . . that.

ROSALIE. Why are you trembling so?

JONATHAN. I'm . . . I'm . . . I'm . . . I'm . . .

ROSALIE. Are you afraid?

JONATHAN. Nnnnnnnnnnnnnnnnnnnno. Whaaaaaaaaaa-why . . . should I . . . be . . . afraid?

ROSALIE. Then why won't you come visit me?

JONATHAN. I . . . I . . . I . . . I . . .

ROSALIE. I don't think you're allowed to go out. That's what I think.

JONATHAN. Nnnn-o. I . . . I can . . . can . . . can . . .

ROSALIE. Why can't you go out, Jonathan? I want to know.

JONATHAN. Nnnnnnnnn-

ROSALIE. Tell me, Jonathan!

JONATHAN. I . . . I . . .

ROSALIE. I said I want to know! *Tell me.*

JONATHAN. I . . . I don't . . . know. I don't know why. I mean, I've . . . nnnnnnnever really thought . . . about going out. I . . . guess it's . . . just natural for me to . . . stay inside. [*He laughs nervously as if that explained everything.*] You see . . . I've got so much to do. I mean, all my sssssstamps and . . . ca-coins and books. The pa-pa-plane might fffffly overhead while I was was going downstairs. And then thhhhere are . . . the plants ta-to feeeeeeed. And I enjoy vvvery much wa . . . watching you and all yyyyyyour chil-dren. I've . . . really got so ma-many things . . . to . . . do. Like . . . like my future, for instance. Ma-Mother says I'm going to be great. That's . . . that's . . . that's what she . . . says. I'm going to be great. I sssswear. Of course, she doesn't know ex-actly what I'm . . . going to be great *in* . . . so she sits every afternoon for . . . for two hours and thinks about it. Na-na-naturally I've . . . got to be here when she's thinking in case she . . . thinks of the answer. Otherwise she might forget and I'd never know . . . what I'm ga-going to be great in. You . . . see what I mean? I mean, I've . . . I've ggggggot so many things to do I . . . just couldn't possibly get *anything* done if I ever . . . went . . . out-side. [*There is a silence.* JONATHAN *stares at* ROSALIE *as if he were hoping that might answer her question sufficiently. She stares back at him as if she knows there is more.*] Besides, Mother locks the front door.

ROSALIE. I thought so.

JONATHAN. No! You-you don't understand. It's not what you think. She doesn't lock the door to kaka-keep me in, which would be malicious. She . . . locks the door so I can't get out, which is for my own good and therefore . . . beneficent.

CUCKOO CLOCK [*From the master bedroom*]. Cuckoo! Cuckoo! Cuckoo!

ROSALIE. What's that?

JONATHAN [*Fearfully*]. A warning.

ROSALIE. What do you mean, a warning?

JONATHAN. A warning that you have to go. Your time is up.

ROSALIE. My time is what?

JONATHAN. Your time is up. You have to go. Now. At once. Right away. You can't stay any longer. You've got to go!

ROSALIE. Why?

JONATHAN [*Puzzled: as if this were the first time the question had ever occurred to him*]. I don't really know.

CUCKOO CLOCK [*Louder*]. Cuckoo! Cuckoo! Cuckoo! [JONATHAN *freezes in terror.* ROSALIE *looks at him calmly.*]

ROSALIE. Why did your mother ask me to come up here?

JONATHAN. What?

ROSALIE. Why did your mother ask me—?

JONATHAN. So I . . . I could meet you.

ROSALIE. Then why didn't you ask me yourself? Something's wrong around here, Jonathan. I don't understand why you didn't ask me yourself.

JONATHAN. Ma-Mother's so much better at those things.

CUCKOO CLOCK [*Very loudly*]. CUCKOO! CUCKOO! CUCKOO!

JONATHAN. You've got to get out of here! That's the third warning. [*He starts to push her toward the door.*]

ROSALIE. Will you call me on the phone?

JONATHAN. Please, you've got to go!

ROSALIE. Instead of your mother telling me to come, will you come and get me yourself? Will you at least call me? Wave to me?

JONATHAN. Yes-yes—I'll do that. Now get out of here!

ROSALIE. I want you to promise to come and see me again.

JONATHAN. Get out!

ROSALIE [*Coyly*]. Promise me.

JONATHAN. GET OUT! [*He pushes her toward the door.*]

ROSALIE. Why do you keep looking at that door?

JONATHAN [*Almost in tears*]. *Please.*

ROSALIE. Why do you keep looking at that door?

JONATHAN. *Please!* You've got to go before it's too late!

ROSALIE. There's something very wrong here. I want to see what's behind that door. [*She starts toward the master bedroom.* JONATHAN *throws his arms about her legs and collapses at her feet, his face buried against her thighs.*]

JONATHAN [*Sobbing uncontrollably*]. I love you. [ROSALIE *stops dead in her tracks and stares down at Jonathan.*]

ROSALIE. What did you say?

JONATHAN. I-I-I llllllove you. I love you, I love you, I love you I—
The CUCKOO CLOCK *screams, cackles, and goes out of its mind, its call ending in a crazed, strident rasp as if it had broken all its springs, screws, and innards. The door to the master bedroom opens.* MADAME ROSEPETTLE *appears.*

JONATHAN [*Weakly*]. *Too late.*

MADAME ROSEPETTLE. Two warnings are enough for any man. Three are enough for any woman. The cuckoo struck three times and then a fourth and still she's here. May I ask why?

ROSALIE. You've been listening at the keyhole, haven't you!

MADAME ROSEPETTLE. I'm talking to my son, harlot!

ROSALIE. What did you say!

MADAME ROSEPETTLE. Harlot, I called you! Slut, scum, sleazy prostitute catching and caressing children and men. Stroking their hearts. I've seen you.

ROSALIE. What are you talking about?

MADAME ROSEPETTLE. Blind man's buff with the children in the garden. The redheaded one—fifteen, I think. Behind the bush while the others cover their eyes. Up with the skirt, one-two-three and it's done. Don't try to deny it. I've seen you in action. I know your kind.

ROSALIE. That's a lie!

MADAME ROSEPETTLE. Life is a lie, my sweet. Not words but Life itself. Life in all its ugliness. It builds green trees that tease your eyes and draw you under them. Then when you're there in the shade and you breathe in and say, "Oh God, how beautiful," that's when the bird on the branch lets go his droppings and hits you on the head. Life, my sweet, beware. It isn't what it seems. I've seen what it can do. I've watched you dance.

ROSALIE. What do you mean by that?

MADAME ROSEPETTLE. Don't try to deny it. I've watched you closely and I know what I see. You danced too near him and you let him do too much. I saw you rub your hand across the back of his neck. I saw you laugh and look closely in his eyes. I'll bet you even told him he was the only one. How many, I wonder, have you told that to? I saw you let him stroke you with his hairy paw and saw you smile. I fancy your thighs must have fairly trembled. It was, my dear, obscene, lewd, disgusting, and quite disgraceful. Everyone was staring at you and yet you went right on. Don't try to deny it. Words will only make it worse. It would be best for all concerned if you left at once and never came again. I will keep the story of your dancing quiet. Good day. MADAME ROSEPETTLE *turns to leave.* ROSALIE *does not move.*]

ROSALIE. Why don't you let Jonathan out of his room?

MADAME ROSEPETTLE [*Sharply*]. Who!?

ROSALIE. Jonathan.

MADAME ROSEPETTLE. Who!?

ROSALIE. Your son.

MADAME ROSEPETTLE. You mean Albert? Is that who you mean? Albert?

JONATHAN. Pa-pa-please do-don't.

MADAME ROSEPETTLE. Is that who you mean, slut? H'm? Speak up? Is that who you mean?

ROSALIE. I mean your son.

MADAME ROSEPETTLE. *I don't let him out because he is my son.* I don't let him out because his skin is as white as fresh snow and he would burn if the sun struck him. I don't let him out because outside there are trees with birds sitting on their branches waiting for him to walk beneath. I don't let him out because you're there, waiting behind the bushes with your skirt up. I don't let him out because he is *susceptible.* That's why. Because he is *susceptible.* Susceptible to trees and to sluts and to sunstroke.

ROSALIE. Then why did you come and get me?

MADAME ROSEPETTLE. Because, my dear, my stupid son has been watching you through that stupid telescope he made. Because, in short, he wanted to meet you and I, in short, wanted him to know what you were really like. Now that he's seen, you may go.

ROSALIE. And if I choose to stay? [*Pause.*]

MADAME ROSEPETTLE [*Softly: slyly*]. Can you cook?

ROSALIE. Yes.

MADAME ROSEPETTLE. How well?

ROSALIE. Fairly well.

MADAME ROSEPETTLE. Not good enough! My son is a connoisseur. A connoisseur, do you hear? I cook him the finest foods in the world. Recipes no one knows exist. Food, my sweet, is the finest of arts. And since you can't cook you are artless. You nauseate my son's aesthetic taste. Do you like cats?

ROSALIE. Yes.

MADAME ROSEPETTLE. What kind of cats?

ROSALIE. Any kind of cats.

MADAME ROSEPETTLE. Alley cats?

ROSALIE. Especially alley cats.

MADAME ROSEPETTLE. I thought so. Go, my dear. Find yourself some weeping willow and set yourself beneath it. Cry of your lust for my son and wait, for a mocking bird waits above to deposit his verdict on your whorish head. My son is as white as fresh snow and you are tainted with sin. You are garnished with garlic and turn our tender stomachs in disgust.

ROSALIE. What did you come to Havana for?

MADAME ROSEPETTLE. To find *you!*

ROSALIE. And now that you've found me . . . ?

MADAME ROSEPETTLE. I throw you out! I toss you into the garbage can! If you'd have left on time I'd have told the sordid details of your dance when you were gone instead of to your face. But it makes no difference. I heard everything, you know. So don't try to call. The phone is in my room . . . and *no one goes into my room but me.*

She stares at ROSALIE *for a moment, then exits with a flourish. * ROSALIE *and* JONATHAN *move slowly toward each other. When they are almost together* MADAME ROSEPETTLE *reappears.*

One more thing. If, by some chance, the eleventh child named Cynthia turns out to be a Siamese cat, give it to me. I too pay well. [MADAME ROSEPETTLE *turns toward her room.* ROSALIE *starts toward the door.* JONATHAN *grabs her hand in desperation.*]

JONATHAN [*In a whisper*]. Come back again. Pa-please . . .
come back again. [*For a moment* ROSALIE *stops and looks at*
JONATHAN. *But* MADAME ROSEPETTLE *stops too, and turning,
looks back at both of them, a slight smile on her lips.* ROSALIE,
sensing her glance, walks toward the door, slipping from JONA-
THAN'S *outstretched hands as she does. The lights fade about*
JONATHAN, *alone in the center of the room.*]

Curtain.

SCENE 3

The hotel room at night, one week later. JONATHAN *is alone in the living room. He is sitting in a chair near the fish bowl, staring at nothing in particular with a particularly blank expression on his face. A clock is heard ticking softly in the distance. For an interminably long time it continues to tick while* JONATHAN *sits in his chair, motionless. After a while the ticking speeds up almost imperceptibly and soon after, laughter is heard. At first it is a giggle from the rear of the theater, then a cough from the side, then a self-conscious laugh from the other side, then a full gusty belly-roar from all corners of the theater. Soon the entire world is hysterical. Cuban drums begin to beat. Fireworks explode. Orgiastic music is heard.*

JONATHAN *continues to sit, motionless. Only his eyes have begun to move. The clock continues to tick. The laughter grows louder: the laughter of the insane. Suddenly* JONATHAN *leaps up and rushes to the French windows, his fingers pressed against his ears. He slams the French windows shut. The noises stop.* JONATHAN *closes his eyes and sighs with relief. The French windows sway unsteadily on their hinges. They tip forward. They fall to the floor. They shatter. The laughter returns.*

JONATHAN *stares down at them in horror. The* VENUS'-FLYTRAPS *grow larger and growl.*

VENUS'-FLYTRAPS [*Viciously*]. Grrrrrrr. [*The* PIRANHA FISH *stares hungrily from its bowl.*]

49

ROSALINDA THE FISH [*More viciously*]. Grarrgh! [*The* FLYTRAPS *lunge at Jonathan but he walks dazedly past, unaware of their snapping petals, and goes out to the edge of the balcony. He stares out in complete bewilderment. The laughter and music of a carnival, the sounds of people dancing in the streets fill the air. He looks down at them sadly. Meekly he waves. The sounds immediately grow softer and the people begin to drift away. He watches as they leave. Behind him the* FLYTRAPS *keep growing and reaching out for him, but of this he is unaware. He only stands at the railing, looking down. A last lingering laugh is heard somewhere in the distance, echoing.*]

The door to the suite opens.

FIRST VOICE [*From outside the door*]. Are you sure this is the room?

SECOND VOICE [*Also outside*]. This is the room, all right. [JONATHAN *hides behind one of the* FLYTRAPS *and watches.*]

THIRD VOICE. And she wants all this stuff in here?

FOURTH VOICE. That's what she said.

FIFTH VOICE. Seems strange to me.

SECOND VOICE. Well don't worry about it. Just do it. After all . . . she tips very well.

THIRD VOICE. If you do what she wants.

FOURTH VOICE. Yes. If you do what she wants.

ALL TOGETHER. Well . . . shall we?

They enter. The voices, we discover, belong to the BELLBOYS, *now dressed as waiters. They enter in order.*

BELLBOY NUMBER ONE [*Carrying a small, round table*]. She said to put it here, I think. [*He sets the table down in the center of the room. The lights slowly begin to fade as an overhead spot begins to illuminate the table.*]

BELLBOYS NUMBER TWO AND THREE [*Carrying chairs in their arms*]. And these here. [*They set one chair on either side of the table.*]

BELLBOY NUMBER FOUR [*Carrying an ice bucket with a huge bottle of champagne in it*]. And the champagne here. [*He sets the ice bucket on the floor between the two chairs at the rear of the table.*]

BELLBOY NUMBER TWO. But what about the candles?

BELLBOY NUMBER THREE. And the glasses?

BELLBOY NUMBER FOUR. And the one wilting rose?

Enter BELLBOY NUMBER FIVE *carrying a tray with two champagne glasses on it, two flickering candles, and a flower vase with one wilting rose protruding.*

BELLBOY NUMBER FIVE. I've got them here.

BELLBOY NUMBER ONE [*Placing a tablecloth on the table*]. Then everything is set.

BELLBOY NUMBER TWO. Just the way she wanted it.

BELLBOY NUMBER THREE. *Exactly* the way she wanted it.

BELLBOY NUMBER FIVE. *Specifically* wanted it. [*He finishes setting the glasses, candles, and flower vase.*]

BELLBOY NUMBER ONE. Yes. Everything is set.

BELLBOY NUMBER FOUR. No. Something is missing.

OTHERS. What!

BELLBOY NUMBER FOUR. We have forgotten something.

OTHERS. Forgotten *what?*

BELLBOY NUMBER FOUR. Well, it seems that we have forgotten the— [*He is interrupted by the sound of a Viennese waltz playing softly, romantically in the background.*]

BELLBOY NUMBER ONE. Oh, I'm sorry. I guess I didn't tell you. She said she'd take care of the music herself.

The lights fade in the room and only the table is lit. The BELLBOYS *disappear into the shadows. The music grows in brilliance.* THE COMMODORE *and* MADAME ROSEPETTLE *waltz into the room. A spot of light follows them about the floor.*

THE COMMODORE. How lovely it was this evening, madame, don't you think? [*She laughs softly and demurely and discretely lowers her eyes. They waltz about the floor.*] How gentle the wind was, madame. And the stars, how clear and bright they were, don't you think? [*She blushes with innocence. They dance on.*] And the moon, madame, shining across the water, lighting the yachts, anchored, so silent and white and clean, waiting for the wind to come and fill their great, clean, white sails again. How poetic it was. How pure, madame. How innocent . . . don't you think? [*She turns her face away and smiles softly. They begin to whirl about the floor.*] Ah, the waltz. How exquisite it is, madame, don't you think? One-two-three, one-two-three, one-two-three. Ahhhhh, madame, how classically simple. How mathematically simple. How stark; how strong . . . how romantic . . . how sublime. [*She giggles girlishly. They whirl madly about the floor.*] Oh, if only Madame knew how I've waited for this moment. If only Madame knew how long. How this week, these nights, the nights we shared together on my yacht; the warm, wonderful nights, the almost-perfect nights, the would-have-been-perfect nights had it not been for the crew peeking through the portholes. Ah, those nights, madame, those nights; almost alone but never quite; but now, tonight, at last, we *are* alone. And now, madame, now we are ready for romance. For the night was made for Love. And tonight, madame . . . we will love.

MADAME ROSEPETTLE [*With the blush of innocence*]. Oh, Commodore, how you do talk. [*They whirl about the room as the lilting rhythm of the waltz grows and sweeps on and on.*]

THE COMMODORE [*Suavely*]. Madame, may I kiss you?

MADAME ROSEPETTLE. Why?

THE COMMODORE [*After recovering from the abruptness of the question; with forced suaveness*]. Your lips . . . are a thing of beauty.

MADAME ROSEPETTLE. My lips, Commodore, are the color of blood. [*She smiles at him. He stares blankly ahead. They dance on.*] I must say, you dance exceptionally well . . . for a man your age.

THE COMMODORE [*Bristling*]. I dance with *you*, madame. That is why I dance well. For to dance with you, madame—is to hold you.

MADAME ROSEPETTLE. Well, I don't mind your holding me, Commodore, but at the moment you happen to be holding me too tight.

THE COMMODORE. I hold you too dear to hold you too tight, madame. I hold you close, that is all. And I hold you close in the hope that my heart may feel your heart beating.

MADAME ROSEPETTLE. One-two-three, one-two-three. You're not paying enough attention to the music, Commodore. I'm afraid you've fallen out of step.

THE COMMODORE. Then lead me, madame. Take my hand and lead me wherever you wish. For I would much rather think of my words than my feet.

MADAME ROSEPETTLE [*With great sweetness*]. Why certainly, Commodore. Certainly. If that is what you want . . . it will be my pleasure to oblige. [*They switch hands and she begins to lead him about the floor. They whirl wildly about, spinning faster than they had when* THE COMMODORE *led.*]

MADAME ROSEPETTLE. Beautiful, isn't it, Commodore? The waltz. The Dance of Lovers. I'm so glad you enjoy it so much. [*With a gay laugh she whirls him around the floor. Suddenly he puts his arms about her shoulders and leans close to kiss her. She pulls back.*] Commodore! You were supposed to spin just then. When I squeeze you in the side it means *spin!*

THE COMMODORE [*Flustered*]. I . . . I thought it was a sign of affection. [*She laughs*].

MADAME ROSEPETTLE. You'll learn. [*She squeezes him in the side. He spins about under her arm.*] Ah, you're learning. [*He continues to spin around and around, faster and faster like a runaway top while* MADAME ROSEPETTLE, *not spinning at all, leads him about the floor, a wild smile of ecstasy spreading over her face.*]

THE COMMODORE. Ho-ho, ho-ho. Stop. I'm dizzy. Dizzy. Stop, please. Stop. Ho-ho. Stop. Dizzy. Ho-ho. Stop. Too fast. Slow. Slower. Stop. Ho-ho. Dizzy. Too dizzy. Weeeeeee! [*And then, without any warning at all, she grabs him in the middle of a spin and kisses him. Her back is to the audience, so* THE COMMODORE'S *face is visible. At first he is too dizzy to realize that his motion has been stopped. But shortly he does, and his first expression is that of shock. But the kiss is long and the shock turns into perplexity and then, finally, into panic; into fear. He struggles*

*desperately and breaks free from her arms, gasping wildly for air.
He points weakly to his chest.*]

THE COMMODORE [*Gasping*]. Asthma. [*His chest heaves as he
gulps in air.*] Couldn't breathe. Lungs bad. Asthmatic. Nose stuffed,
too. Sinus condition. Couldn't get any air. [*He gasps for air. She
starts to walk toward him, slowly.*] Couldn't get any . . . air.
[*She nears him. Instinctively he backs away.*] You . . . you sur-
prised me . . . you know. Out . . . of breath. Wasn't . . . ready
for that. Didn't . . . expect you to kiss me.

MADAME ROSEPETTLE. I know. That's why I did it. [*She laughs
and puts her arm tenderly about his waist.*] Perhaps you'd prefer
to sit down for a while, Commodore. Catch your breath, so to
speak. Dancing can be so terribly tiring . . . when you're growing old. Well, if you like, Commodore, we could just sit and talk.
And perhaps . . . sip some pink champagne, eh? Champagne?

THE COMMODORE. Ah, champagne. [*She begins to walk with
him toward the table.*]

MADAME ROSEPETTLE. And just for the two of us.

THE COMMODORE. Yes. The two of us. Alone.

MADAME ROSEPETTLE [*With a laugh*]. Yes. All alone.

THE COMMODORE. At last.

MADAME ROSEPETTLE. With music in the distance.

THE COMMODORE. A waltz.

MADAME ROSEPETTLE. A *Viennese* waltz.

THE COMMODORE. The Dance of Lovers. [*She takes his hand,
tenderly.*]

MADAME ROSEPETTLE. Yes, Commodore. The Dance of Lovers. [*They look at each other in silence.*]

THE COMMODORE. Madame, you have won my heart. And easily.

MADAME ROSEPETTLE. No, Commodore. You have lost it. *Easily.* [*She smiles seductively. The room darkens till only a single spot of light falls upon the table set in the middle of the room. The waltz plays on.* MADAME ROSEPETTLE *nods to* THE COMMODORE *and he goes to sit. But before he can pull his chair out, it slides out under its own power. He places himself and the chair slides back in, as if some invisible waiter had been holding it in his invisible hands.* MADAME ROSEPETTLE *smiles sweetly and, pulling out her chair herself, sits. They stare at each other in silence. The waltz plays softly.* THE COMMODORE *reaches across the table and touches her hand. A thin smile spreads across her lips. When finally they speak, their words are soft: the whispered thoughts of lovers.*]

MADAME ROSEPETTLE. Champagne?

THE COMMODORE. Champagne.

MADAME ROSEPETTLE. Pour?

THE COMMODORE. Please. [*She lifts the bottle out of the ice bucket and pours with her right hand, her left being clasped firmly in* THE COMMODORE'*s passionate hands. They smile serenely at each other. She lifts her glass. He lifts his. The music swells.*]

MADAME ROSEPETTLE. A toast?

THE COMMODORE. To you.

MADAME ROSEPETTLE. No, Commodore, to you.

THE COMMODORE. No, madame. To us.

MADAME ROSEPETTLE
THE COMMODORE $\Big\}$ [*Together*]. To us. [*They raise their*]
glasses. They gaze wistfully into each other's eyes. The music
builds to brilliance. THE COMMODORE clinks his glass against
MADAME ROSEPETTLE's glass. The glasses break.]

THE COMMODORE [*Furiously mopping up the mess.*] Pardon,
madame! Pardon!

MADAME ROSEPETTLE [*Flicking some glass off her bodice*]. Pas
de quoi, monsieur.

THE COMMODORE. J'étais emporté par l'enthousiasme du moment.

MADAME ROSEPETTLE [*Extracting pieces of glass from her lap*].
Pas de quoi. [THE COMMODORE *suddenly stretches across the table
in order to stop the puddle of champagne from spilling over onto*
MADAME ROSEPETTLE's *glass-spattered lap. His elbow knocks over
the flower vase. The table is inundated with water.*]

THE COMMODORE [*Gasping*]. Mon dieu!

MADAME ROSEPETTLE [*Watching with a serenely inane grin, as
the water pours over the edge of the table and onto her dress*].
Pas de quoi, monsieur. Pas de quoi.
She snaps her fingers gaily. Immediately a WAITER *appears from
the shadow with a table in his hands. It is already covered with
a tablecloth, two champagne glasses, two candelabra (the candles
already flickering in them), and a vase with one wilting rose protruding. Another* WAITER *whisks the wet table away. The new
table is placed. The* WAITERS *disappear into the shadows.*

MADAME ROSEPETTLE [*Lifting the bottle of champagne out of
the ice bucket*]. Encore?

THE COMMODORE. S'il vous plaît. [*She pours. They lift their glasses in a toast. The music swells again.*] To us.

MADAME ROSEPETTLE. To us, monsieur . . . Commodore. [*They clink their glasses lightly.* THE COMMODORE *closes his eyes and sips.* MADAME ROSEPETTLE *holds her glass before her lips, poised but not touching, waiting. She watches him. Then she speaks softly.*] Tell me about yourself.

THE COMMODORE. My heart is speaking, madame. Doesn't it tell you enough?

MADAME ROSEPETTLE. Your heart, monsieur, is growing old. It speaks with a murmur. Its words are too weak to understand.

THE COMMODORE. But the feeling, madame, is still strong.

MADAME ROSEPETTLE. Feelings are for animals, monsieur. Words are the specialty of Man. Tell me what your heart has to say.

THE COMMODORE. My heart says it loves you.

MADAME ROSEPETTLE. And how many others, monsieur, has your heart said this to?

THE COMMODORE. None but you, madame. None but you.

MADAME ROSEPETTLE. And you, monsieur, with all your money and your worldly ways, how many have loved you?

THE COMMODORE. Many, madame.

MADAME ROSEPETTLE. How many, monsieur?

THE COMMODORE. Too many, madame

MADAME ROSEPETTLE. So I, alone, am different?

THE COMMODORE. You alone . . . do I love.

MADAME ROSEPETTLE. And pray, monsieur, just what is it that I've done to make you love me so?

THE COMMODORE. Nothing, madame. And that is why. You are a strange woman, you see. You go out with me and you know how I feel. Yet, I know nothing of you. You disregard me, madame, but never discourage. You treat my love with indifference . . . but never disdain. You've led me on, madame. That is what I mean to say.

MADAME ROSEPETTLE. I've led you to my room, monsieur. That is all.

THE COMMODORE. To me, that is enough.

MADAME ROSEPETTLE. I know. That's why I did it. [*The music swells. She smiles distantly. There is a momentary silence.*]

THE COMMODORE [*With desperation*]. Madame, I must ask you something. Now. Because in all the days I've been with you there's been something I've wanted to know, but you've never told me so now, right now, I must ask. Madame, why are you here?

MADAME ROSEPETTLE [*She pauses before answering*]. I have to be somewhere, don't I?

THE COMMODORE. But why here, where I am? Why in Havana?

MADAME ROSEPETTLE. You flatter yourself, monsieur. I am in Havana only because Havana was in my way. . . . I think I'll move on tomorrow.

THE COMMODORE. For . . . home?

MADAME ROSEPETTLE [*Laughing slightly*]. Only the very young and the very old have homes. I am neither. And I have none.

THE COMMODORE. But . . . surely you must come from somewhere.

MADAME ROSEPETTLE. Nowhere you've ever been.

THE COMMODORE. I've been many places.

MADAME ROSEPETTLE [*Softly*]. But not many enough. [*She picks up her glass of champagne and sips, a distant smile on her lips.*]

THE COMMODORE [*With sudden, overwhelming, and soul-rendering passion*]. Madame, don't go tomorrow. Stay. My heart is yours.

MADAME ROSEPETTLE. How much is it worth?

THE COMMODORE. A fortune, madame.

MADAME ROSEPETTLE. Good. I'll take it in cash.

THE COMMODORE. But the heart goes with it, madame.

MADAME ROSEPETTLE. And you with the heart, I suppose?

THE COMMODORE. Forever.

MADAME ROSEPETTLE. Sorry, monsieur. The money's enticing and the heart would have been nice, but you, I'm afraid, are a bit too bulky to make it all worth while.

THE COMMODORE. You jest, madame.

MADAME ROSEPETTLE. I never jest, monsieur. There isn't enough time.

THE COMMODORE. Then you make fun of my passion, madame, which is just as bad.

MADAME ROSEPETTLE. But monsieur, I've never taken your passion seriously enough to make fun of it. [*There is a short pause.* THE COMMODORE *sinks slowly back in his seat.*]

THE COMMODORE [*Weakly, sadly*]. Then why have you gone out with me?

MADAME ROSEPETTLE. So that I might drink champagne with you tonight.

THE COMMODORE. That makes no sense.

MADAME ROSEPETTLE. It makes *perfect* sense.

THE COMMODORE. Not to me.

MADAME ROSEPETTLE. It does to me.

THE COMMODORE. But *I* don't understand. And I *want* to understand.

MADAME ROSEPETTLE. Don't worry, Commodore. You will.

THE COMMODORE. When?

MADAME ROSEPETTLE. Soon.

THE COMMODORE. How soon?

MADAME ROSEPETTLE. Very soon. [*He stares at her in submissive confusion. Suddenly, with final desperation, he grabs her*

*hands in his and, leaning across the table, kisses them passionately,
sobbingly. Then in a scarcely audible whisper she says.]* Now.

THE COMMODORE. Madame . . . I love you. Forever. Don't you
understand? [*He kisses her hand again. A smile of triumph spreads
across her face.*] Oh, your husband . . . He must have been . . .
a wonderful man . . . to deserve a woman such as you. [*He sobs
and kisses her hands again.*]

MADAME ROSEPETTLE [*Nonchalantly*]. Would you like to see
him?

THE COMMODORE. A snapshot?

MADAME ROSEPETTLE. No. My husband. He's inside in the
closet. I had him stuffed. Wonderful taxidermist I know. H'm?
What do you say, Commodore? Wanna peek? He's my very favorite trophy. I take him with me wherever I go.

THE COMMODORE [*Shaken; not knowing what to make of it*].
Hah-hah, hah-hah. Yes. Very good. Very funny. Sort of a . . . um
. . . *white elephant*, you might say.

MADAME ROSEPETTLE. *You* might say.

THE COMMODORE. Well, it's . . . certainly very . . . coura-
geous of you, a . . . a woman still in mourning, to . . . to be able
to laugh at what most other women wouldn't find . . . well, shall
we say . . . funny.

MADAME ROSEPETTLE. Life, my dear Commodore, is *never*
funny. It's grim! It's there every morning breathing in your face
the moment you open your red baggy eyes. Worst of all, it follows
you wherever you go. Life, Mr. Roseabove, is a husband hanging
from a hook in the closet. Open the door without your customary
cup of coffee and your whole day's shot to hell. But open the door
just a little ways, sneak your hand in, pull out your dress, and

your day is made. Yet he's still there, and waiting—your husband, hanging by his collar from a hook, and sooner or later the moth balls are gone and you've got to clean house. It's a bad day, Commodore, when you have to stare Life in the face, and you find he doesn't smile at all; just hangs there . . . with his tongue sticking out.

THE COMMODORE. I . . don't find this . . . very funny.

MADAME ROSEPETTLE. Sorry. I was hoping it would give you a laugh.

THE COMMODORE. I don't think it's funny at all. And the reason that I don't think it's funny at all is that it's not my kind of joke. One must respect the dead.

MADAME ROSEPETTLE. Then tell me, Commodore . . . why not the living, too? [*Pause. She lifts out the bottle of champagne and pours herself some more.*]

THE COMMODORE [*Weakly, with a trace of fear*]. How . . . how did he die?

MADAME ROSEPETTLE. Why, I killed him of course. Champagne? [*She smiles sweetly and fills his glass. She raises hers in a toast.*] To your continued good health. [*He stares at her blankly. The music swells in the background.*] Ah, the waltz, monsieur. Listen. The waltz. The Dance of Lovers. Beautiful . . . *don't you think?* [*She laughs and sips some more champagne. The music grows to brilliance. THE COMMODORE starts to rise from his chair.*]

THE COMMODORE. Forgive me, madame. But . . . I find I must leave. Urgent business calls. Good evening. [*He tries to push his chair back, but for some reason it will not move. He looks about in panic. He pushes frantically. It does not move. It is as if the invisible waiter who had come and slid the chair out when he went to sit down now stood behind the chair and held it in so*]

he could not get up. And as there are arms on the chair, THE
COMMODORE *cannot slide out the side.* MADAME ROSEPETTLE
smiles.]

MADAME ROSEPETTLE. Now you don't *really* want to leave . . .
do you, Commodore? After all, the night is still so young . . .
and you haven't even seen my husband yet. We shared such love
for so many years, Commodore, I would so regret if you had to
leave without seeing him. And believe me, Commodore, the
expression on his face is easily worth the price of admission. So
please, Commodore, won't you reconsider? Won't you stay? . . .
just for a little while? [*He stares at her in horror. He tries once
more to push his chair back. But the chair does not move. He
sinks down into it weakly. She leans across the table and tenderly
touches his hand.*] Good. I knew you'd see it my way. It would
have been such a shame if you'd have had to leave. For you see,
Commodore, we are in a way united. We share something in
common . . . you and I. . . . We share desire. For you desire
me, with love in your heart. While I, my dear Commodore . . .
desire your heart. [*She smiles sweetly and sips some more champagne.*] How simple it all is, in the end. [*She rises slowly from
her chair and walks over to him. She runs her hands lovingly
through his hair and down the back of his neck.*] Tell me, Commodore, how would you like to hear a little story? A bedtime story?
A fairy tale full of handsome princes and enchanted maidens;
full of love and joy and music; tenderness and charm? Would
you like to hear it, Commodore? Eh? It's my very favorite story,
you see . . . and since you're my very favorite commodore, it
seems only appropriate that I tell it to you . . . *don't you think?*

THE COMMODORE. No. I . . . I don't think so.

MADAME ROSEPETTLE. Good. Then I'll tell it. I never leave a
place without telling it to at least one person. How very lucky you
are. How very lucky. [*The light on the table dims slightly.*

MADAME ROSEPETTLE *walks slowly away. A spot of light follows her as she goes. The light on the table fades more.* THE COMMODORE *sits, motionless.*]

His name was Albert Edward Robinson Rosepettle III. How strange and sad he was. All the others who had come to see me had been tall, but he was short. They had been rich, while he was poor. The others had been handsome, but Albert, poor Albert, he was as ugly as a humid day . . . [*She laughs sadly, distantly.*] and just about as wet, too. Oh, he was a fat bundle of sweat, Mr. Roseabove. He was nothing but one great torrent of perspiration. Winter and summer, spring and fall, Albert was dripping wet. And he wasn't very good-looking either. He had a large green wart on the very tip of his nose and he talked with a lisp and walked with a limp and his left ear, which was slightly larger than his right, was as red as a bright red beet. He was round and wet and hideous and I never could figure out how he ever got such a name as Albert Edward Robinson Rosepettle III.

Oh, I must have been very susceptible indeed to have married Albert. I *was* twenty-eight and that *is* a susceptible year in a woman's life. And of course I *was* a virgin, but still I— Oh, stop blushing, Mr. Roseabove. I'm not lying. It's all true. Part of the cause of my condition, I will admit, was due to the fact that I still hadn't gone out with a man. But I am certain, Mr. Roseabove, I am certain that despite your naughty glances my virtue would have remained unsoiled, no matter what. Oh, I had spoken to men. (Their voices are gruff.) And in crowded streets I had often brushed against them. (Their bodies, I found, are tough and bony.) I had observed their ways and habits, Mr. Roseabove. Even at that tender age I had the foresight to realize I must know what I was up against. So I watched them huddled in hallways, talking in nervous whispers and laughing when little girls passed by. I watched their hands in crowded buses and even felt their feeling elbows on crowded streets. And then, one night, when I was walking home I saw a man standing in a window. I saw him take his contact lenses out and his hearing aid out of his ear. I saw him take his teeth out of his thin-lipped mouth and drop them into a smiling glass of water. I saw him lift his snow-white hair off of his wrinkled white head and place it on a gnarled wooden hat tree. And then I saw him take his clothes off. And when he was done and didn't move but stood and stared at a full-length mirror whose glass he had covered with towels, then I went home and wept.

And so one day I bolted the door to my room. I locked myself inside, bought a small revolver just in case, then sat at my window and watched what went on below. It was not a pretty sight. Some men came up to see me. I don't know how they got my name. But I have heard that once a woman reaches womanhood her fragrance wanders out into the world and her name becomes the common property of Men. Just as a single drop of blood will attract a distant school of sharks, so Man, without any introduction, can catch the scent of any woman anywhere and find her home. That is what I've heard. No place then is safe from them. You cannot hide. Your name is known and there is nothing left that can be done. I suppose if you like you can lock your door. It doesn't keep them away; just keeps them out. I locked my door. They came and knocked. I did not let them in.

> "Hello in there," they said.
>
> "Hello in there,
>
> My name is Steven.
>
> Steven S. (for Steven) Steven.
>
> One is odd
>
> But two is even.
>
> I know you're hot
>
> So I'm not leavin'."

. . . or something like that.

[*Short pause.*] But they all soon left anyway. I think they caught the scent of a younger woman down the hall. And so I stayed inside my room and listened to the constant sound of feet disappearing down the stairs. I watched a world walk by my window; a world of lechery and lies and greed. I watched a world walk by and I decided not to leave my room until this world came to me, *exactly* as I wanted it.

One day Albert came toddling up the stairs. He waddled over to my room, scratched on the door and said, in a frail and very frightened voice, "Will you please marry me?" And so I did. It was as simple as that. [*Pause. Then distantly.*] I still wonder why I did it though. I still wonder why. [*Short pause.Then with a laugh of resignation.*] I don't really know why. I guess it just seemed like the right thing to do. Maybe it's because he was the first one who ever asked me. No, that's not right. . . . Perhaps it's because he was so ugly and fat; so unlike everything I'd ever heard a husband should be. No, that doesn't make much sense either. . . . Perhaps it's . . . yes, perhaps it's because one look at Albert's round, sad face and I knew he could be mine . . . that no matter where he went, or whom he saw, or what he did, Albert would be mine, all mine—mine to love, mine to live with, mine to kill; my husband, my lover, my own . . . *my very own.*

And so we were wed. That night I went to bed with a man for the first time in my life. The next morning I picked up my mattress and moved myself into another room. Not that there was something wrong with Albert. Oh, no! He was *quite* the picture of health. His pudgy, pink flesh bouncing with glee. Oh, how easily is Man satisfied. How easily is his porous body saturated with "fun." All he asks is a little sex and a little food and there he is, asleep with a smile and snoring. Never the slightest regard for you, lying in bed next to him, your eyes open wide. No, he stretches his legs and kicks you in the shins; stretches his arms and smacks you in the eye. Lean over to kiss him good night and he'll belch in your face till all your romantic dreams are dissolved in an image of onions, garlic, and baked Boston beans. Oh, how considerate is Man when he's had his fill of sex. How noble, how magical, how marvelous is Love.

And so, I picked up my mattress and left his room. For as long as I stayed in his room I was not safe. After all, he was a total stranger to me. We'd only met the day before and I knew far too little. But now that we were married I had time to find out more. His life was a mystery and his mind contained too many secrets. In short, I was in danger. So I decided to find out certain things. A few of these were: what had he done before we'd ever met, what had he wanted to do, what did he still want to do, what was he doing about it? What did he dream about while he slept? What did he think about when he stared out the window? What did he think about when I wasn't near?

These were the things that concerned me most. And so I began to watch him closely.

My plan worked best at night, for that was when he slept. . . . I would listen at my door until I heard his door close. Then I'd tiptoe out and watch him through his keyhole. When his lights went out I'd open up his door and creep across the floor to his bed. And that, Mr. Roseabove, is where I stayed, every night— next to him; my husband, my "Love." I never left his side, never took my eyes from his sleeping face. I dare you to find me a wife who's as devoted as that. [*She laughs.*] And so I watched. I listened to him breathe. My ear was a stethoscope that recorded the fluctuations of his dream life. I put my ear next to his mouth so I might hear the slightest word that he might say, the slightest word that would betray his sleeping, secret thoughts. I listened for my name upon his lips. I listened for a word of "love." I listened for anything, but he only snored, and smiled, and slept on and on. So every night I waited and listened, and every morning when the dawn came I left, knowing no more than when I'd come.

A month later I found that I was pregnant. It had happened that first horrible night. How like Albert to do something like that. I fancy he knew it was going to happen all the time, too. I do believe he planned it that way. One night, one shot, one chance in a lifetime and bham! you've had it. It takes an imaginative man to miss. It takes someone like Albert to do something like that. But yet, I never let on. Oh, no. Let him think I'm simply getting fat, I said. And that's the way I did it, too. I, nonchalantly putting on weight; Albert nonchalantly watching my belly grow. If he knew what was happening to me he never let me know it. He was as silent as before. It was only at night that he changed. Only at night while he slept that something strange suddenly

occurred. I found that the smile on his face had become a grin.
[*Pause.*]

Twelve months later my son was born. He was so overdue
that when he came out he was already teething. He bit the index
finger off the poor doctor's hand and snapped at the nurse till
she fainted. I took him home and put him in a cage in the
darkest corner of my room. But still I—

THE COMMODORE. Was it a large cage?

MADAME ROSEPETTLE. What?

THE COMMODORE. Was his cage large? I hope it was. Otherwise
it wouldn't be very comfortable.

MADAME ROSEPETTLE. I'm sorry. Did I say cage? I meant crib.
I put him in a crib and set the crib in a corner of my room
where my husband would not see him. For until I found out
exactly why he'd married me, until I understood his dreams, until
that time I was not safe, and until that time I would not tell him
that his son had been born. And so I went on as if nothing had
happened. At night I'd slip into his room and watch him while
he slept. He still refused to say a word. And yet, somehow, his
grin seemed broader. And then, one night, he made that noise.
At first I thought it just some . . . sort of snore. But then I
listened closely. I was wrong. I know it sounds peculiar, Mr.
Roseabove, but I swear it's true. While I looked on, Albert slept
. . . and giggled. [*Pause.*]

Shortly after that, Rosalinda came. She was one of Albert's
many secretaries. Since I'd married him, you see, he'd become
a multibillionaire. My influence, of course. We'd moved from
a four-room flat to a four-acre mansion. Albert had taken the
north wing, my son and I the south. But when Rosalinda came,
things changed. I've always felt there was something star-crossed
about those two, for she was the only person I ever met who was
equally as ugly as he. It seems her mother had once owned a

laundromat and, at the tender age of five, Rosalinda, a curious child, had taken an exploratory trip through the mangler. The result of the trip being that her figure took on an uncanny resemblance to nothing less than a question mark.

Well, naturally I never let on that I knew she had come. When she walked in front of me I looked straight through her. When she spoke I looked away. I flatly refused to recognize her presence. I simply set an extra place at the table and cooked a little bit more. Though Albert watched me like a naughty boy anxious to see his mother's reaction to a mischievous deed, I disregarded his indiscretions and continued my life as if nothing had changed. If he were searching for some sign of annoyance, I never showed it. If he were waiting to be scolded *I* was waiting for him to give up. So at night, instead of preparing one, I prepared two beds. Instead of fluffing one pillow I fluffed up two and straightened an extra pair of sheets. I said good night as politely as I could and left them alone—the hunchback and my husband, two soulmates expressing their souls through sin. And while they lay in bed I listened at the keyhole. And when they slept I crept in and listened more. Albert had begun to speak!

After months of listening for some meager clue he suddenly began to talk in torrents. Words poured forth and I, like some listening sponge, soaked them up and stayed for more. At last he was talking in his sleep and I was there, sinking farther and farther into his brain, gaining more and more control. He told her things he never told to me. Words of passion and love. He told her how he worshiped the way she cooked; how he worshiped the way she talked; how he'd worshiped the way she'd looked when he'd first met her; even the way she looked now. And this to a hunchback. A hunchback! To a hideous, twisted slut sleeping in sin with him! Words he never told to me. I ask you, Mr. Roseabove, how much is a woman supposed to take?

But the signs of regret were beginning to show. And oh, how I laughed when I found out: when I saw how tired he'd begun to look, when I noticed how little he ate; how little he spoke; how slowly he seemed to move. It's funny, but he never slept any more. I could tell by his breathing. And through the keyhole at night I could see his large, round, empty eyes shining sadly in the dark. [*Pause.*]

Then one night he died. One year after she had come he passed on. The doctors don't know why. His heart, they said, seemed fine. It was as large a heart as they'd ever seen. And yet he died. At one o'clock in the morning his heart stopped beating. [*She laughs softly.*] But it wasn't till dawn that she discovered he was dead. [*She starts to laugh louder.*]

Well, don't you get it? Don't you catch the irony, the joke? What's wrong with you!? He died at one. At ONE O'CLOCK IN THE MORNING!! DEAD!!! Yet she didn't know he was dead till dawn. [*She laughs again, loudly.*]

Well don't you get the point? The point of this whole story? What is wrong with you? He was lying with her in bed for nearly six hours, *dead,* and she never knew it! What a lover he must have been! WHAT A LOVER! [*She laughs uproariously but stops when she realizes he's not laughing with her.*]

Well don't you see? Their affair, their sinfulness—it never even existed! He tried to make me jealous but there was nothing to be jealous of. His love was sterile! He was a child. He was weak. He was impotent. He was *mine!* Mine all the time, even when he was in bed with another, even in death . . . *he was mine!* [THE COMMODORE *climbs up in his chair and crawls over his arm rest. He begins to walk weakly toward the door.*] Don't tell me you're leaving, Commodore. Is there something wrong? [THE COMMODORE *walks weakly toward the door, then runs the last part of the way. In panic he twists the doorknob. The doorknob comes off. He falls to the ground.*] Why Commodore, you're on your knees! *How romantic.* Don't tell me you're going to ask me to marry you again? Commodore, you're trembling. What's wrong? Don't tell me you're afraid that I'll accept?

THE COMMODORE [*Weakly*]. I . . . I-I . . . feel . . . sa-sorry for your . . . ssssson . . . that's . . . all I can . . . sssssay.

MADAME ROSEPETTLE. And I feel sorrier for you! For you are *nothing!* While my son is mine. His skin is the color of fresh

snow, his voice is like the music of angels, and his mind is pure.
For he is safe, Mr. Roseabove, and it is *I* who have saved him.
Saved him from the world beyond that door. The world of you.
The world of his father. A world waiting to devour those who
trust in it; those who love. A world vicious under the hypocrisy of
kindness, ruthless under the falseness of a smile. Well, go on,
Mr. Roseabove. Leave my room and enter your world again—
your sex-driven, dirt-washed waste of cannibals eating each other
up while they pretend they're kissing. Go, Mr. Roseabove, enter
your blind world of darkness. My son shall have only light! [*She
turns with a flourish and enters her bedroom.* THE COMMODORE
*stares helplessly at the doorknob in his hand. Suddenly the door
swings open, under its own power.* THE COMMODORE *crawls out.
The door closes behind him, under its own power. From outside
can be heard the sound of a church bell chiming. The bedroom
door reopens and* MADAME ROSEPETTLE *emerges wearing an im-
mense straw hat, sunglasses, tight toreador pants, and a short
beach robe. She carries a huge flashlight. She is barefoot. She
tiptoes across the floor and exits through the main door. The
church bell chimes thirteen times.*]

JONATHAN *emerges from behind the* VENUS'-FLYTRAPS. *He runs
to the door, puts his ear to it, then races back to the balcony and
stares down at the street below. Carnival lights flash weirdly
against the night sky and laughter drifts up. The* VENUS'-FLYTRAPS
*reach out to grab him but somehow he senses their presence and
leaps away in time.*

VENUS'-FLYTRAPS [*Gruffly*]. Grrrrrrr! [*He walks dazedly into the
living room.*]

ROSALINDA THE FISH. [*Snarlingly*]. Snarrrrrrrl! [*The* VENUS'-
FLYTRAPS *have grown enormous. Their monstrous petals wave
hungrily in the air while they growl.* JONATHAN *stares at them
fearfully, the laughter below growing stronger all the while.
Suddenly he runs to the wall and smashes the glass case that
covers the fire axe. He takes out the axe. He advances cautiously
toward the* FLYTRAPS. *He feints an attack, they follow his move-*

ments. He bobs, they weave. It is a cat-and-mouse game of death. Suddenly JONATHAN *leaps upon them and hacks them apart till they fall to the floor, writhing, then dead.* JONATHAN *stands above them, victorious, panting, but somehow seeming to breathe easier. Slowly he turns and looks at the fish bowl. His eyes seem glazed, his expression insanely determined. He walks slowly toward the fish bowl. . . . There are three knocks on the door. He does not hear them. He raises his axe.*]

The door opens. ROSALIE *enters. She is dressed in an absurdly childish pink dress with crinolines and frills—the picture of innocence, the picture of a girl ten years old. Her shoes are black leather pumps and she wears short girlish-pink socks. Her cheeks have round circles of rouge on them—like a young girl might have who had never put on make-up before.*

ROSALIE. Jonathan! Jonathan! What *have* you done? [JONATHAN *stops. He does not look at her but stares at the fish bowl.*] Jonathan! Put down that silly axe. You might hurt yourself. [*He still does not answer but stares at the bowl. He does not lower the axe.*] Jonathan! [*Slowly he turns and faces her.*]

JONATHAN. I killed it.

ROSALIE. Ssh. Not so loudly. Where'd you put her body?

JONATHAN [*Pointing to the* PLANTS]. There.

ROSALIE. Where? I don't see a body. Where is she?

JONATHAN. Who?

ROSALIE. Your mother.

JONATHAN. I haven't killed my mother. I've killed her plants. The ones I used to feed. I've chopped their hearts out.

ROSALIE [*With an apologetic laugh*]. I thought you'd . . .

killed your mother. [The PIRANHA FISH *giggles*. JONATHAN *turns and stares at it again. He starts to move toward it, slowly.*]

ROSALIE. Jonathan, stop. [*He hesitates, as if he is uncertain what to do. Slowly he raises the axe.*] Jonathan! [*He smashes the axe against the fish bowl. It breaks. The fish screams.*]

ROSALINDA THE FISH [*Fearfully*]. AAIEEEEEEEEEEEEEEE!

ROSALIE. Now look at the mess you've made.

JONATHAN. Do you think it can live without water?

ROSALIE. What will your mother say when she gets back?

JONATHAN. Maybe I should hit it again. Just in case. [*He strikes it again.*]

ROSALINDA THE FISH [*Mournfully*]. UGHHHHHHH! [JONA-THAN *stares in horror at the dead* FISH. *He drops the axe and turns away, sickened and weak.* ROSALIE *walks over and touches him gently, consolingly, on the arm.*]

ROSALIE. There's something bothering you, isn't there? [*Pause —coyly.*] What's-a matter, Jonathan? [JONATHAN *does not answer at first but stares off into space frightened, bewildered.*]

JONATHAN [*Weakly*]. I never thought I'd see you again. I never thought I'd talk to you again. I never thought you'd come.

ROSALIE. Did you really think that?

JONATHAN. She told me she'd never let you visit me again. She said no one would *ever* visit me again. She told me I had seen enough.

ROSALIE. But I had a key made.

JONATHAN. She . . . she hates me.

ROSALIE. What?

JONATHAN. She doesn't let me do anything. She doesn't let me listen to the radio. She took the tube out of the television set. She doesn't let me use her phone. She makes me show her all my letters before I seal them. She doesn't—

ROSALIE. Letters? What letters are you talking about?

JONATHAN. Just . . . letters I write.

ROSALIE. To *whom?*

JONATHAN. To people.

ROSALIE. *What* people?

JONATHAN. Oh . . . various people.

ROSALIE. Other girls? Could they be to other girls, by any chance?

JONATHAN. No. They're just to people. No people in particular. Just people in the phone book. Just names. I do it alphabetically. That way, someday, I'll be able to cover everyone. So far I've covered all the "A's" and "B's" up to Barrera.

ROSALIE. What is it you say to them? Can you tell me what you say to them . . . or is it private? Jonathan, just what do you say to them!?

JONATHAN. Mostly I just ask them what they look like. [*Pause. Suddenly he starts to sob in a curious combination of laughter and tears.*] But I don't think she ever mails them. She reads them, then takes them out to mail. But I don't think she ever does. I'll bet she just throws them away. Well if she's not going to mail them, why does she say she will? I . . . I could save the stamps. Why must she lie to me? Why doesn't she just say she's not going to mail them? Then I wouldn't have to wait for letters every day.

ROSALIE. Guess why I had this key made.

JONATHAN. I'll bet she's never even mailed one. From Abandono to Barrera, not one.

ROSALIE. Do you know why I had this key made? Do you know why I'm wearing this new dress?

JONATHAN. She doesn't let me stand in the window at noon because the sun is too strong. She doesn't let me stand in the window at night when the wind is blowing because the air is too cold. And today she told me she's going to nail shutters over the windows so I'll never have to worry about being bothered by the sun or the wind again.

ROSALIE. Try and guess why I'm all dressed up.

JONATHAN. She tells me I'm brilliant. She makes me read and reread books no one's ever read. She smothers me with blankets at night in case of a storm. She tucks me in so tight I can't even get out till she comes and takes my blankets off.

ROSALIE. Stop talking about that and pay attention to me!

JONATHAN. She says she loves me. Every morning, before I even have a chance to open my eyes, there she is, leaning over my bed, breathing in my face and saying, "I love you, I love you."

ROSALIE. Jonathan, isn't my dress pretty?

JONATHAN. But I heard everything tonight. I heard it all when she didn't know I was here. [*He stares off into space, bewildered.*]

ROSALIE. What's the matter? [*He does not answer.*] Jonathan, what's the matter?

JONATHAN. But she must have known I was here. She *must* have known! I mean . . . where could I have gone? (*Pause.*) But . . . if that's the case . . . *why did she let me hear?*

ROSALIE. Jonathan, I do wish you'd pay more attention to me. Here, look at my dress. You can even touch it if you like. Guess how many crinolines I have on. Guess why I'm wearing such a pretty, new dress. *Jonathan!*

JONATHAN [*Distantly*]. Maybe . . . it didn't make any difference to her . . . whether I heard or not. [*He turns suddenly to her and hugs her closely. She lets him hold her, then she steps back and away from him. Her face looks strangely old and determined under her girlish powder and pinkness.*]

ROSALIE. Come with me.

JONATHAN. What?

ROSALIE. Leave and come with me.

JONATHAN [*Fearfully*]. Where?

ROSALIE. Anywhere.

JONATHAN. What . . . wha . . . what do you mean?

ROSALIE. I mean, let's leave. Let's run away. Far away. Tonight. Both of us, together. Let's run and run. Far, far away.

JONATHAN. You . . . mean, leave?

ROSALIE. Yes. *Leave.*

JONATHAN. Just like that?

ROSALIE. *Just like that.*

JONATHAN. But . . . but . . . but . . .

ROSALIE. You want to leave, don't you?

JONATHAN. I . . . I don't . . . don't know. I . . . I . . .

ROSALIE. What about the time you told me how much you'd like to go outside, how you'd love to walk by yourself, anywhere you wanted?

JONATHAN. I . . . I don't . . . know.

ROSALIE. Yes you do. Come. Give me your hand. Stop trembling so. Everything will be all right. Give me your hand and come with me. Just through the door. Then we're safe. Then we can run far away, somewhere where she'll never find us. Come, Jonathan. It's time to go. I've put on a new dress just for the occasion. I even had a key made so I could come and get you.

JONATHAN. There are others you could take.

ROSALIE. But I don't love them. [*Pause.*]

JONATHAN. You . . . you *love* me?

ROSALIE. Yes, Jonathan. I love you.

JONATHAN. Wha-wha-why?

ROSALIE [*Softly*]. Because you watch me every night.

JONATHAN. Well . . . can't we stay here?

ROSALIE. *No.*

JONATHAN. Wha-wha-whhhhy?

ROSALIE. Because I want you *alone.* [JONATHAN *turns from her and begins to walk about the room in confusion.*] I want you, Jonathan. Do you understand what I said? *I want you for my husband.*

JONATHAN. I . . . I . . . can't, I mean, I . . . I want to . . . go with you very much but I . . . I don't think . . . I can. I'm . . . sorry. [*He sits down and holds his head in his hands, sobbing quietly.*]

ROSALIE. What time will your mother be back?

JONATHAN. Na—not for a while.

ROSALIE. Are you sure?

JONATHAN. Ya-yes.

ROSALIE. Where is she?

JONATHAN. The usual place.

ROSALIE. What do you mean, "The usual place"?

JONATHAN [*With a sad laugh*]. The beach. [ROSALIE *looks at* JONATHAN *quizzically.*] She likes to look for people making love. Every night at midnight she walks down to the beach searching for people lying on blankets and making love. When she finds them she kicks sand in their faces and walks on. Sometimes it takes her as much as three hours to chase everyone away. [ROSALIE *smiles slightly and walks toward the master bedroom.* JONATHAN *freezes in fear. She puts her hand on the doorknob.*]

JONATHAN. WHAT ARE YOU DOING!? [*She smiles at him over her shoulder. She opens the door.*] STOP! You can't go in there! STOP! [*She opens the door completely and beckons to him.*]

ROSALIE. Come.

JONATHAN. Close it. Quickly!

ROSALIE. Come, Jonathan. Let's go inside.

JONATHAN. Close the door!

ROSALIE [*With a laugh*]. You've never been in here, have you?

JONATHAN. No. And you can't go in, either. No one can go in there but Mother. It's her room. Now close the door! [*She flicks on the light switch. No lights go on.*]

ROSALIE. What's wrong with the lights?

JONATHAN. There are none. . . . Mother's in mourning. [*ROSALIE walks into the room and pulls the drapes off the windows. Weird colored lights stream in and illuminate the bedroom in wild, distorted, nightmarish shadows and lights. They blink on and off, on and off. It's all like some strange, macabre fun house in an insane amusement park. Even the furniture in the room seems grotesque and distorted. The closet next to the bed seems peculiarly prominent. It almost seems to tilt over the bed.*]

JONATHAN [*Still in the main room*]. What have you done!? [*ROSALIE walks back to the door and smiles to him from within the master bedroom.*] What have you done?

ROSALIE. Come in, Jonathan.

JONATHAN. GET OUT OF THERE!

ROSALIE. Will you leave with me?

JONATHAN. I can't!

ROSALIE. But you want to, don't you?

JONATHAN. Yes, yes, I want to, but I told you . . . I . . . I . . . I can't. I can't! Do you understand? I can't! Now come out of there.

ROSALIE. Come in and get me.

JONATHAN Rosalie, *please.*

ROSALIE [*Bouncing on the bed*]. My, what a comfortable bed.

JONATHAN. [*Horrified*]. GET OFF THE BED!

ROSALIE. What soft, fluffy pillows. I think I'll take a nap.

JONATHAN. Rosalie, *please listen to me.* Come out of there. You're not supposed to be in that room. Please come out. Rosalie, *please.*

ROSALIE. Will you leave with me if I do?

JONATHAN. Rosalie . . . ? I'll . . . I'll show you my stamp collection if you'll promise to come out.

ROSALIE. Bring it in here.

JONATHAN. Will you come out then?

ROSALIE. Only if you bring it in here.

JONATHAN. But I'm not allowed to go in there.

ROSALIE [*Poutingly*]. Then I shan't come out!

JONATHAN. You've got to!

ROSALIE. Why?

JONATHAN. Mother will be back.

ROSALIE. She can sleep out there. [ROSALIE *yawns*.] I think I'll take a little nap. This bed is so comfortable. Really, Jonathan, you should come in and try it.

JONATHAN. MOTHER WILL BE BACK SOON!

ROSALIE. Give her your room, then, if you don't want her to sleep on the couch. I find it very nice in here. Good night. [*Pause*.]

JONATHAN. If I come in, will you come out?

ROSALIE. If you don't come in I'll never come out.

JONATHAN. And if I do?

ROSALIE. Then I may.

JONATHAN. What if I bring my stamps in?

ROSALIE. Bring them and find out. [*He goes to the dresser and takes out the drawer of stamps. Then he takes out the drawer of coins.*]

JONATHAN. I'm bringing the coins, too.

ROSALIE. How good you are, Jonathan. [*He takes a shelf full of books.*]

JONATHAN. My books, too. How's that? I'll show you my books

and my coins and my stamps. I'll show you them all. Then will you leave?

ROSALIE. Perhaps. [*He carries them all into the bedroom and sets them down next to the bed. He looks about fearfully.*]

ROSALIE. What's wrong?

JONATHAN. I've never been in here before.

ROSALIE. It's nothing but a room. There's nothing to be afraid of. [*He looks about doubtfully.*]

JONATHAN. Well, let me show you my stamps. I have one billion, five—

ROSALIE. Later, Jonathan. We'll have time. Let me show you something first.

JONATHAN. What's that?

ROSALIE. You're trembling.

JONATHAN. What do you want to show me?

ROSALIE. There's nothing to be nervous about. Come. Sit down.

JONATHAN. What do you want to show me?

ROSALIE. I can't show you if you won't sit down.

JONATHAN. I don't want to sit down! [*She takes hold of his hand. He pulls it away.*]

ROSALIE. Jonathan!

JONATHAN. You're sitting on Mother's bed.

ROSALIE. Then let's pretend it's my bed.

JONATHAN. It's not your bed!

ROSALIE. Come, Jonathan. Sit down here next to me.

JONATHAN. We've got to get out of here. Mother might come.

ROSALIE. Don't worry. We've got plenty of time. The beach is full of lovers.

JONATHAN. How do you know?

ROSALIE. I checked before I came. [*Pause.*]

JONATHAN. Let . . . let me show you my coins.

ROSALIE. Why are you trembling so?

JONATHAN. Look, we've got to get out! Something terrible will happen if we don't.

ROSALIE. Then leave with me.

JONATHAN. The bedroom?

ROSALIE. The hotel. The island. Your mother. Leave with me, Jonathan. Leave with me now, before it's too late.

JONATHAN. I . . . I . . . I . . .

ROSALIE. I love you, Jonathan, and I won't give you up. I want you . . . all for myself. Not to share with your mother, but for me, alone . . . to love, to live with, to have children by. I want you, Jonathan. You, whose skin is softer and whiter than any-one's I've ever known; whose voice is quiet and whose love is in every look of his eye. I want you, Jonathan, and I won't give you up. [*Short pause.*]

JONATHAN [*Softly, weakly*]. What do you want me to do?

ROSALIE. Forget about your mother. Pretend she never existed and look at me. Look at my eyes, Jonathan; my mouth, my hands, my skirt, my legs. Look at me, Jonathan. Are you still afraid?

JONATHAN. I'm not afraid. [*She smiles and starts to unbutton her dress.*] What are you doing!? No! [*She continues to unbutton her dress.*]

ROSALIE. Your mother is strong, but I am stronger. [*She rises and her skirt falls about her feet. She stands in a slip and crinolines.*] I don't look so pink and girlish any more, do I? [*She laughs.*] But you want me anyhow. You're ashamed but you want me anyhow. It's written on your face. And I'm very glad. Because I want you. [*She takes off a crinoline.*]

JONATHAN. PUT IT ON! *Please*, put it back on!

ROSALIE. Come, Jonathan. [*She takes off another crinoline.*] Lie down. Let me loosen your shirt.

JONATHAN. No . . . NO . . . NO! STOP! *Please*, stop! [*She takes her last crinoline off and reaches down to take off her socks. The lights outside blink weirdly. Wild, jagged music with a drum beating in the background is heard.*]

ROSALIE. Don't be afraid, Jonathan. Come. Lie down. Everything will be wonderful. [*She takes her socks off and lies down in her slip. She drops a strap over one shoulder and smiles.*]

JONATHAN. Get off my mother's bed!

ROSALIE. I want you, Jonathan, all for my own. Come. The bed is soft. Lie here by my side.

She reaches up and takes his hand. Meekly he sits down on the edge of the bed. The closet door swings open suddenly and the

corpse of Albert Edward Robinson Rosepettle III tumbles for-
ward stiffly and onto the bed, his stone-stiff arms falling across
Rosalie's *legs, his head against her side.* Jonathan, *too terrified*
to scream, puts his hand across his mouth and sinks down onto
the bed, almost in a state of collapse. Outside the music screams.

Rosalie. Who the hell is this!?

Jonathan. It-it-it-it . . . it . . . it's . . .

Rosalie. What a stupid place to keep a corpse. [*She pushes*
him back in the closet and shuts the door.] Forget it, Jonathan.
I put him back in the closet. Everything's fine again.

Jonathan. It's . . . it's . . . it's my . . . my . . . my . . .

Rosalie [*Kneeling next to him on the bed and starting to*
unbutton his shirt.] It's all right, Jonathan. It's all right. Sshh.
Come. Let me take off your clothes.

Jonathan [*Still staring dumbly into space*]. It's . . . it's my
. . . ffffather.
The closet door swings open again and the corpse falls out, this
time his arms falling about Rosalie's *neck.* Jonathan *almost*
swoons.

Rosalie. Oh, for God's sake. [*She pushes the corpse off the bed*
and onto the floor.] Jonathan . . . ? LISTEN TO ME, JONA-
THAN! STOP LOOKING AT HIM AND LOOK AT ME!
[*He looks away from his father, fearfully, his mouth open in*
terror.] I love you, Jonathan, and I want you *now.* Not later and
not as partner with your mother but now and by myself. I want
you, Jonathan, as my husband. I want you to lie with me, to
sleep with me, to be with me, to kiss me and touch me, to live
with me, *forever.* Stop looking at him! He's dead! Listen to me.
I'm alive. I want you for my husband! Now help me take my slip

off. Then you can look at my body and touch me. Come, Jonathan. Lie down. I want you forever.

JONATHAN. Ma-Mother was right! You *do* let men do anything they want to you.

ROSALIE. Of course she was right! Did you really think I was that sweet and pure? Everything she said was right. [*She laughs.*] Behind the bushes and it's done. One-two-three and it's done. Here's the money. Thanks. Come again. Hah-hah! Come again! [*Short pause.*] So what!? It's only you I love. They make no difference.

JONATHAN. You're dirty! [*He tries to get up but can't, for his father is lying in front of his feet.*]

ROSALIE. No, I'm not dirty. I'm full of love and womanly feelings. I want children. Tons of them. I want a husband. Is that dirty?

JONATHAN. You're dirty!

ROSALIE. No. I'm pure. I want no one but you. I renounce all past lovers. They were mistakes. I confess my indiscretions. Now you know all so I'm pure again. Take off your clothes.

JONATHAN. NO!

ROSALIE. Forget about your father. Drop your pants on top of him, then you won't see his face. Forget about your mother. She's gone. Forget them both and look at me. Love is so beautiful, Jonathan. Come and let me love you; tonight and forever. Come and let me keep you mine. Mine to love when I want, mine to kiss when I want, mine to have when I want. Mine. All mine. So come, Jonathan. Come and close your eyes. It's better that way. Close your eyes so you can't see. Close your eyes and let me lie with you. Let me show you how beautiful it is . . . love.

[*She lies back in bed and slowly starts to raise her slip.* JONATHAN *stares at her legs in horror. Then, suddenly, he seizes her crumpled skirt and throws it over her face. He smothers her to death. . . . At last he rises and, picking up his box of stamps, dumps the stamps over her limp body. He does the same with his coins and finally his books, until at last she is buried. Then, done, he throws his hands over his eyes and turns to run. But as he staggers past the corpse of his father, his father's lifeless arms somehow come to life for an instant and, reaching out, grab Jonathan by the feet.* JONATHAN *falls to the floor. For a moment he lies there, stretched across his father's body, too terrified to move. But a soft, ethereal-green light begins to suffuse the room and heavenly harp music is heard in the air. As if his body had suddenly become immortal and weightless,* JONATHAN *rises up from the floor and with long, slow, dreamlike steps (like someone walking under water), he floats through the bedroom door and drifts across the living room, picking up his telescope on the way. He floats out to the balcony and begins to scan the sky. The harp music grows louder and more paradisiacal: Debussy in Heaven. While under the harp music, soft, muffled laughter can be heard; within the bedroom, within the living room, from the rear of the theater, laughter all about.*]

His mother tiptoes into the living room. Her air is awry, her hat is on crooked, her blouse hangs wrinkled and out of her pants. Her legs are covered with sand.

MADAME ROSEPETTLE. Twenty-three couples. I annoyed twenty-three couples, all of them coupled in various positions, all equally distasteful. It's a record, that's what it is. It's a record! [*Breathing heavily from excitement she begins to tuck in her blouse and straighten her hair. She notices the chaotic state of the room. She shrieks slightly.*] What has happened!? [*She notices the* PLANTS.] My plants! [*She notices the* FISH.] Rosalinda! Great gods, my fish has lost her water! ALBERT! ALBERT! [*She searches about the room for her* SON. *She sees him standing on the porch.*] Ah, there you are. Edward, what has been going on during my brief absence? What are you doing out here when Rosalinda is lying in there dead? DEAD!? Oh God, dead. Robinson, answer me. What are you looking for? I've told you there's nothing out there. This place is a madhouse. That's what it is. A madhouse. [*She turns and walks into her bedroom. An airplane is heard flying in the distance.* JONATHAN *scans the horizon frantically. The plane grows nearer. Jonathan follows it with his telescope. It flies overhead. It begins to circle about. Wildly, desperately, Jonathan waves his arms to the plane. . . . It flies away.*]

MADAME ROSEPETTLE *re-enters the room.*

Robinson! I went to lie down and I stepped on your father! I lay down and I lay on some girl. Robinson, there is a woman on my bed and I do believe she's stopped breathing. What is more, you've buried her under your fabulous collection of stamps, coins, and books. I ask you, Robinson. As a mother to a son I ask you. *What is the meaning of this?*

Blackout and Curtain.

DRAMABOOKS
(Plays)

WHEN ORDERING, please use the Standard Book Number consisting of the publisher's prefix, 8090–, plus the five digits following each title. (Note that the numbers given in this list are for paperback editions only. Many of the books are also available in cloth.)

MERMAID DRAMABOOKS

Christopher Marlowe (Tamburlaine the Great, Parts I & II, Doctor Faustus, The Jew of Malta, Edward the Second) (0701–0)

William Congreve (Complete Plays) (0702–9)

Webster and Tourneur (The White Devil, The Duchess of Malfi, The Atheist's Tragedy, The Revenger's Tragedy) (0703–7)

John Ford (The Lover's Melancholy, 'Tis Pity She's a Whore, The Broken Heart, Love's Sacrifice, Perkin Warbeck) (0704–5)

Richard Brinsley Sheridan (The Rivals, St. Patrick's Day, The Duenna, A Trip to Scarborough, The School for Scandal, The Critic) (0705–3)

Camille and Other Plays (Scribe: A Peculiar Position, The Glass of Water; Sardou: A Scrap of Paper; Dumas: Camille; Augier: Olympe's Marriage) (0706–1)

John Dryden (The Conquest of Granada, Parts I & II, Marriage à la Mode, Aureng-Zebe) (0707–X)

Ben Jonson Vol. 1 (Volpone, Epicoene, The Alchemist) (0708–8)

Oliver Goldsmith (The Good Natur'd Man, She Stoops to Conquer, An Essay on the Theatre, A Register of Scotch Marriages) (0709–6)

Jean Anouilh Vol. 1 (Antigone, Eurydice, The Rehearsal, Romeo and Jeannette, The Ermine) (0710–X)

Let's Get a Divorce! and Other Plays (Labiche: A Trip Abroad, and Célimare; Sardou: Let's Get a Divorce!; Courteline: These Cornfields; Feydeau: Keep an Eye on Amélie; Prévert: A United Family; Achard: Essays on Feydeau) (0711–8)

Jean Giraudoux Vol. 1 (Ondine, The Enchanted, The Madwoman of Chaillot, The Apollo of Bellac) (0712–6)

Jean Anouilh Vol. 2 (Restless Heart, Time Remembered, Ardèle, Mademoiselle Colombe, The Lark) (0713–4)

Henrik Ibsen: The Last Plays (Little Eyolf, John Gabriel Borkman, When We Dead Awaken) (0714–2)

Ivan Turgenev (A Month in the Country, A Provincial Lady, A Poor Gentleman) (0715–0)

George Farquhar (The Constant Couple, The Twin-Rivals, The Recruiting Officer, The Beaux Stratagem) (0716–9)

Jean Racine (Andromache, Britannicus, Berenice, Phaedra, Athaliah) (0717–7)

The Storm and Other Russian Plays (The Storm, The Government Inspector, The Power of Darkness, Uncle Vanya, The Lower Depths) (0718–5)

Michel de Ghelderode: Seven Plays Vol. 1 (The Ostend Interviews, Chronicles of Hell, Barabbas, The Women at the Tomb, Pantagleize, The Blind Men, Three Players and a Play, Lord Halewyn) (0719–3)

Lope de Vega: Five Plays (Peribáñez, Fuenteovejuna, The Dog in the Manger, The Knight from Olmedo, Justice Without Revenge) (0720–7)

Calderón: Four Plays (Secret Vengeance for Secret Insult, Devotion to the Cross, The Mayor of Zalamea, The Phantom Lady) (0721–5)

Jean Cocteau: Five Plays (Orphée, Antigone, Intimate Relations, The Holy Terrors, The Eagle with Two Heads) (0722–3)

Ben Jonson Vol. 2 (Every Man in His Humour, Sejanus, Bartholomew Fair) (0723–1)

Port-Royal and Other Plays (Claudel: Tobias and Sara; Mauriac: Asmodée; Copeau: The Poor Little Man; Montherlant: Port-Royal) (0724–X)

Edwardian Plays (Maugham: Loaves and Fishes; Hankin: The Return of the Prodigal; Shaw: Getting Married; Pinero: Mid-Channel; Granville-Barker: The Madras House) (0725–8)

Alfred de Musset: Seven Plays (0726–6)

Georg Büchner: Complete Plays and Prose (0727–4)

Paul Green: Five Plays (Johnny Johnson, In Abraham's Bosom, Hymn to the Rising Sun, The House of Connelly, White Dresses) (0728–2)

François Billetdoux: Two Plays (Tchin-Tchin, Chez Torpe) (0729–0)

Michel de Ghelderode: Seven Plays Vol. 2 (Red Magic, Hop, Signor!, The Death of Doctor Faust, Christopher Columbus, A Night of Pity, Piet Bouteille, Miss Jairus) (0730–4)

Jean Giraudoux Vol. 2 (Siegfried, Amphitryon 38, Electra) (0731–2)

Kelly's Eye and Other Plays by Henry Livings (Kelly's Eye, Big Soft Nellie, There's No Room for You Here for a Start) (0732–0)

Gabriel Marcel: Three Plays (Man of God, Ariadne, Votive Candle) (0733–9)

New American Plays Vol. 1 ed. by Robert W. Corrigan (0734–7)

Elmer Rice: Three Plays (Adding Machine, Street Scene, Dream Girl) (0735–5)
The Day the Whores Came Out to Play Tennis . . . by Arthur Kopit (0736–3)
Platonov by Anton Chekhov (0737–1)
Ugo Betti: Three Plays (The Inquiry, Goat Island, The Gambler) (0738–X)
Jean Anouilh Vol. 3 (Thieves' Carnival, Medea, Cécile, Traveler Without Luggage, Orchestra, Episode in the Life of an Author, Catch As Catch Can) (0739–8)
Max Frisch: Three Plays (Don Juan, The Great Rage of Philip Hotz, When the War Was Over) (0740–1)
New American Plays Vol. 2 ed. by William M. Hoffman (0741–X)
Plays from Black Africa ed. by Fredric M. Litto (0742–8)
Anton Chekhov: Four Plays (The Seagull, Uncle Vanya, The Cherry Orchard, The Three Sisters) (0743–6)
The Silver Foxes Are Dead and Other Plays by Jakov Lind (The Silver Foxes Are Dead, Anna Laub, Hunger, Fear) (0744–4)
New American Plays Vol. 3 ed. by William M. Hoffman (0745–2)

THE NEW MERMAIDS

Bussy D'Ambois by George Chapman (1101–8)
The Broken Heart by John Ford (1102–6)
The Duchess of Malfi by John Webster (1103–4)
Doctor Faustus by Christopher Marlowe (1104–2)
The Alchemist by Ben Jonson (1105–0)
The Jew of Malta by Christopher Marlowe (1106–9)
The Revenger's Tragedy by Cyril Tourneur (1107–7)
A Game at Chess by Thomas Middleton (1108–5)
Every Man in His Humour by Ben Jonson (1109–3)
The White Devil by John Webster (1110–7)
Edward the Second by Christopher Marlowe (1111–5)
The Malcontent by John Marston (1112–3)
'Tis Pity She's a Whore by John Ford (1113–1)
Sejanus His Fall by Ben Jonson (1114–X)
Volpone by Ben Jonson (1115–8)
Women Beware Women by Thomas Middleton (1116–6)

SPOTLIGHT DRAMABOOKS

The Last Days of Lincoln by Mark Van Doren (1201–4)
Oh Dad, Poor Dad . . . by Arthur Kopit (1202–2)
The Chinese Wall by Max Frisch (1203–0)
Billy Budd by Louis O. Coxe and Robert Chapman (1204–9)
The Devils by John Whiting (1205–7)
The Firebugs by Max Frisch (1206–5)
Andorra by Max Frisch (1207–3)
Balm in Gilead and Other Plays by Lanford Wilson (1208–1)
Matty and the Moron and Madonna by Herbert Lieberman (1209–X)
The Brig by Kenneth H. Brown (1210–3)
The Cavern by Jean Anouilh (1211–1)
Saved by Edward Bond (1212–X)
Eh? by Henry Livings (1213–8)
The Rimers of Eldritch and Other Plays by Lanford Wilson (1214–6)
In the Matter of J. Robert Oppenheimer by Heinar Kipphardt (1215–4)
Ergo by Jakov Lind (1216–2)
Biography: A Game by Max Frisch (1217–0)
Indians by Arthur Kopit (1218–9)
Narrow Road to the Deep North by Edward Bond (1219–7)

For a complete list of books of criticism and history of the drama, please write to Hill and Wang, 72 Fifth Avenue, New York, New York 10011.